A Writer's Ireland

Also by William Trevor

NOVELS

The Old Boys
The Boarding-House
The Love Department
Mrs Eckdorf in O'Neill's Hotel
Miss Gomez and the Brethren
Elizabeth Alone
The Children of Dynmouth
Other People's Worlds
Fools of Fortune

SHORT STORIES

The Day We Got Drunk on Cake
The Ballroom of Romance
Angels at the Ritz
Lovers of Their Time
Beyond the Pale

William Trevor

A Writer's Ireland

Landscape in Literature

The Viking Press · New York

Frontispiece: Co. Cork landscape

The acknowledgments on p. 180
are an extension of the copyright page

Map drawn by Bryan Woodfield

Copyright © 1984 by William Trevor
All rights reserved

Published in 1984 by The Viking Press
40 West 23rd Street, New York, N.Y. 10010

Library of Congress Catalog Card Number: 83-81754
ISBN 0-670-79082-6

Printed and bound in Spain
Set in Monophoto Bembo
D.L. TO-1190-83

Contents

Introduction

Ireland, the largest island beyond Britain, is situated in the western ocean about one short day's sailing from Wales, but between Ulster and Galloway in Scotland the sea narrows to half that distance. Nevertheless from either side the promontories of the other can be fairly well seen and distinguished on a fine day. The view from this side is rather clear; that from the other, over such a distance, is more vague. This farthest island of the west has Spain parallel to it on the south at a distance of three ordinary days' sailing, Greater Britain on the east, and only the ocean on the west; but on the northern side, at a distance of three days' sailing, lies Iceland, the largest of the islands of the north. Ireland, then, lies parallel to Britain in such a way that if you sail to the west from any British port you will meet Ireland at some point.

from *The History and Topography of Ireland*. Giraldus Cambrensis.
Translated from the Latin by John J. O'Meara.

THE MAP OF Ireland is not unlike a sleeping infant: the rounded head of Ulster, fingers scattered to make the islands and inlets of the West, toes spread out in Dingle and the O'Sullivan country, Carnsore Point the tip of the spine. It's a pleasing, jagged shape, and its places have a ring to them: Ballinskelligs, Mount Melleray, the MacGillycuddy Reeks, Slieve Aughty, Slieve Bloom, Maam Cross, Limavady, Vinegar Hill.

Ireland is a country of uneven surface and rather mountainous. The soil is soft and watery, and there are many woods and marshes. Even at the tops of high and steep mountains you will find pools and swamps. Still there are, here and there, some fine plains, but in comparison with the woods they are indeed small. On the whole the land is low-lying on all sides and along the coast; but further inland it rises up very high to many hills and even high mountains. It is sandy rather than rocky, not only on its circumference, but also in the very interior.

Giraldus of Wales visited Ireland for the first time in 1183 and his topographical map can have been nothing like the symbol of freedom with which, centuries later, the early Irish Free State replaced a royal profile on its postage stamps. As a glimmer of nostalgia, the symbol still twinkles for the exile in bars all over the world: four provinces in different colours, green and red, yellow and blue, on the label of Paddy Whiskey. Divide it ecclesiastically and those quarters become Tuam, Cashel, Dublin and Armagh. Examine it before the Norman invasion and the divisions are more numerous and more interesting. After the Cromwellian settlement it changes again: the real beginning of Ireland's thorny history, land marked out in strict plantations.

7

Ireland's story is its people, the O'Neills and the MacCarthys, the O'Kellys and the O'Connors, the Norman families who became more Irish than the natives, and all the others who arrived and didn't want to go away. That story is endlessly reflected in Ireland's places: in the fallen walls of castles and abbeys, in sorrowful demesnes, in St John Gogarty's Sackville Street that is Sackville Street no more, in the woods and hills where generations of rebels lay low. The story haunts the battleground at Kinsale, and the towers of nervous monks. It has been played out on land and sea, by cliffs and caves, on riverbanks, in fields, over bog and stone.

> The Fort over against the oak-wood,
> Once it was Bruidge's, it was Cathal's,
> It was Aed's, it was Ailill's,
> It was Conaing's, it was Cuilíne's
> And it was Maeldúin's;
> The Fort remains after each in his turn –
> And the kings asleep in the ground.
>
> *The Fort of Rathangan.* Anonymous.
> Translated from the Irish by Kuno Meyer.

This book is not an academic investigation of either Irish literature or the inspiration of landscape. It is a writer's journey, a tour of places which other writers have felt affection for also, or have known excitement or alarm in. Among those others the twelfth-century Giraldus Cambrensis has a special place because in a sense he led the literary way. He was the first commentator to record an appreciation of Irish landscape that sought to include every aspect of his subject, and even extended to a landscape of people. He was the first to leave behind him a picture of medieval life that sparkles with colour and liveliness. He was the first to allow an idiosyncratic wit to play upon factual dullness, transforming and decorating everyday Ireland. He was not always accurate – indeed, so often the opposite that he might be dubbed, as well, Ireland's first fiction writer. But usually, in his claims, he was simply quoting what others had told him, for his credulity was part of his storyteller's genius.

There is in Connacht a village celebrated for a church of Saint Nannan. In olden times there was such a multitude of fleas there that the place was almost abandoned because of the pestilence, and was left without inhabitants, until, through the intercession of Saint Nannan, the fleas were brought to a certain neighbouring meadow. The divine intervention because of the merits of the saint so cleansed the place that not a single flea could ever afterwards be found here. But the number of them in the meadow is so great that it ever remains inaccessible not only to men but also to beasts.

The cocks of Ireland, so Giraldus says, crow differently from other cocks. The wolves of Ireland perversely give birth in December. Near Wicklow there lived a man who 'had all the parts of the human body except the extremeties which were those of an ox'. In Munster there was a well which turned people grey when they washed in its water, and another which deluged the province with rain if anyone touched it or even looked at it. There was a lake island which no woman could step on to without immediately dying. There was a sea island on which human corpses did not putrefy, where men recognized their 'grandfathers, great-grandfathers, and great-great-grandfathers and a long line of ancestors'. Near Cork a stone bled wine every morning, enough 'for the celebration of as many Masses as there are priests to say Mass on that day'. Kildare was found to be the place of most miracles. White peacocks strutted proudly everywhere. In Dublin there was a cross which spoke.

The land is fruitful and rich in its fertile soil and plentiful harvests. Crops abound in the fields, flocks on the mountains, and wild animals in the woods. The island is, however, richer in pastures than in crops, and in grass than in grain. The crops give great promise in the blade, even more in the straw, but less in the ear. The island is rich in pastures and meadows, honey and milk, and wine, but not vineyards. Bede, however, among his other praises of the island says that it is not altogether without vineyards. On the other hand Solinus says that it has no bees.

Detail of a chancel arch, Tuam Cathedral, Co. Galway, late 12th century.

Dun Aengus, a Celtic cliff-fort on Inishmore, the largest of the Aran Islands, off the Galway coast.

The Distant Past

THERE MUST HAVE BEEN a beginning. There must have been someone who arrived long, long before Giraldus, who walked along Irish shores and visited the places of his wonders. A woman it was, he suggests, who may first of all have lingered by the stream which boasted a fish with golden teeth, who rested in the beeless meadows: none other than the grand-daughter of Noah.

> According to the most ancient histories of the Irish, Cesara, the grand-daughter of Noah, hearing that the Flood was about to take place, decided to flee in a boat with her companions to the farthest islands of the West, where no man had yet ever lived. She hoped that the vengeance of the Flood would not reach to a place where sin had never been committed. All the ships of her company were wrecked. Her ship alone, carrying three men and fifty women, survived. It put in at the Irish coast, by chance, one year before the Flood.

But even Giraldus had his doubts (as he did in the end about the bees). He couldn't quite swallow the advent of Noah's grand-daughter, and so speculated no further on the earliest inhabitants of the scenery he had come to examine so hungrily and so affectionately himself. Visions of the distant past were best left where they were, obscure in a fog of too much time.

The first eyes to gaze upon the contours of Ireland were those of wanderers. They had come from what is now Scotland, probably not having had to cross the sea, for the two islands of Britain and Ireland were as likely as not laced together as a single entity. The Ice Age was receding. It was a time for tentative exploration.

The wanderers built their primeval settlements in the north of the land, then journeyed down the rivers and the coast, attracted by fish and birds, as hunters in Ireland have been ever since. They came in peace and caused less trouble than any of their successors, but it is hard to imagine their lives or even their physical appearance. Hard, too, to imagine the landscape they passed through except, inaccurately perhaps, to conjure up the territory of a dream, a forest maze of tree-trunks in mile after mile of stately jungle. Did the explorers experience joy or even relief when the monotony was broken by the torrent of a waterfall or waves lapping over shingle? Emerging above some little creek, did they delight in the blue of the sky? and resting in the darkness did they tell one another the first stories that ever were heard in Ireland, travellers' tales of nature in the raw? Or were they quite unlike that, soulless creatures, kin with the animals they pursued? There are no answers; guesses have to do.

The wanderers' descendants exist for us through their dying. The funeral ceremonies of death, the placating of the gods they came in time to feel a need of, the familiar fear of the unknown: in their huge necropolises there is a flavour of all that, but the people themselves are still elusive. Their wonderlands of stone tease us with the mystery of that faraway megalithic existence, impersonal artefacts imprinted with a permanence that has come to challenge landscape's own.

With time, people do emerge, but in legend that is often clearly far removed from the unvarnished truth. In his *History of Ireland*, Edmund Curtis was wisely vague when he wrote:

> The traditions of the Irish people are the oldest of any race in Europe north and west of the Alps, and they themselves are the longest settled on their own soil. When they learned to write they recorded the tradition that they originally came from northern Spain. The ancient *Leabar Gabála* (the *Book of Invasions*) tells how the three sons of Mileadh of Spain, namely, Heremon, Heber, and Ir, came to Erin about the time of Alexander the Great and conquered the land from the Tuatha Dé Danann. Of the races that were in possession before them, the Tuatha Dé Danann were a superior race, semi-divine in their arts of magic and wizardry, the Firbolg were a race dark, short, and plebeian, the Fomorians were gloomy giants of the sea. From the three sons of Mileadh descended all the royal clans of later Ireland.

The Tuatha Dé Danann, the Firbolg, the Fomorians and the Milesians are fanciful names that belong in a circus of myth and hyperbole brought to Ireland by the Celts, who were themselves very real indeed. Having slipped mysteriously into a European existence, they conquered an area from Delphi in the south to far beyond Abernethy in the north. 'For many years,' wrote Lucretius, 'among the beasts of the earth they led their life.' The Greek geographer, Strabo, described them as 'madly fond of war, high-spirited and quick to battle, but otherwise straightforward and not of evil character'. They were keen drinkers of alcohol, tall and red-haired and boastful, but hospitable in their rough-necked way. Even after they began to organize their tribal, warlike existence in a crudely aristocratic pattern, they continued to be considered barbarians by both Greeks and Romans, and when the civilization of imperial Rome swept through Europe it swept the Celts in front of it. Ireland saved them from the Atlantic.

This remnant of a gypsy empire in the twilight of its day first arrived in Ireland probably about 350 BC. Hillforts were built as a sign of serious intent as the Celts settled down determinedly in the last territory they ever conquered. In a new, meditative mood they found themselves haunted and disturbed by the memorial stones that surrounded them and it was then, with reverence and with awe, that they invented as their predecessors the Firbolg and the Fomorians and the three sons of Mileadh. It was then, too, that they invested with divinity the mythological Tuatha Dé Danann, the Tribes of the Goddess Dana. 'The barbarians have civilized themselves at last,' the superior Romans would no doubt have said.

The Celts recognized the site of the great hillfort at Tara as a holy place as soon as they set eyes on it. Tara's 'Mound of Hostages' is built over a much earlier grave (*c.* 2000 BC), which continued to be used as such during the Bronze Age. A similar pattern is found near Armagh at Navan Fort, which the Celts called Emain Macha. Their contribution to this place, also recognized by them as one of sanctity, was the belief that the goddess Macha was buried there. They made it their capital of the North, as once it may have been before and as, in Christian terms, it has become again.

'A terrible beauty is born,' Yeats wrote very many centuries later, referring to the emergence at last of an Irish nation: the words apply equally well to what happened when the Celts, making Ireland their own, recreated its ghosts. They were already considerable craftsmen and their language had gradually enriched itself. But for the first time – in their new-found tranquillity   skill and imagination fused: their place of survival became the repository of their genius. The cairns and dolmens which tamed them are today part of Ireland's landscape, and their obsession with people of the past has its modern equivalent

Stone with ogham script, Ireland's first venture into literacy.

also. As their long rampage quietened, thought changed its form among a race which had always had such difficulty in finding the discipline necessary for anything more than the rough and tumble of battle and conquest. Their characteristic wildness never deserted the Celts and increasingly now it lent exuberance and dash to their sagas.

Just as, in their particular way, they conserved what they found at Tara and Emain Macha, so the Celts continued the old tradition of the standing stone as a sign of death. Their ogham stones incorporated Ireland's first alphabet, one that was unfortunately neither complex nor elaborate enough to record the stories that enlivened their evening gatherings. In turn these stories were conserved by much later generations, and the thread of connection with the Celts tenuously preserved. The contemporary poet Thomas Kinsella, translating from medieval Irish, tells how Emain Macha received its name:

> There was a very rich landlord in Ulster, Crunniuc mac Agnomain. He lived in a lonely place in the mountains with all his sons. His wife was dead. Once, as he was alone in the house, he saw a woman coming toward him there, and she was a fine woman in his eyes. She settled down and began working at once, as though she were well used to the house. When night came, she put everything in order without being asked. Then she slept with Crunniuc.
>
> She stayed with him for a long while afterward, and there was never a lack of food or clothes or anything else under her care.
>
> Soon, a fair was held in Ulster. Everyone in Ulster, men and women, boys and girls, went to the fair. Crunniuc set out for the fair with the rest, in his best clothes and in great vigour.
>
> 'It would be as well not to grow boastful or careless in anything you say,' the woman said to him.
>
> 'That isn't likely,' he said.
>
> The fair was held. At the end of the day the king's chariot was brought onto the field. His chariot and horses won. The crowd said that nothing could beat those horses.
>
> 'My wife is faster,' Crunniuc said.
>
> He was taken immediately before the king and the woman was sent for. She said to the messenger:
>
> 'It would be a heavy burden for me to go and free him now. I am full with child.'
>
> 'Burden?' the messenger said. 'He will die unless you come.'
>
> She went to the fair, and her pangs gripped her. She called out to the crowd: 'A mother bore each one of you! Help me! Wait till my child is born.'
>
> But she couldn't move them.
>
> 'Very well,' she said. 'A long-lasting evil will come out of this on the whole of Ulster.'

The hill of Tara, Co. Meath. Here, traditionally, the Irish kings were crowned.

'What is your name?' the king said.

'My name, and the name of my offspring,' she said, 'will be given to this place. I am Macha, daughter of Sainrith mac Imbaith.'

Then she raced the chariot. As the chariot reached the end of the field, she gave birth alongside it. She bore twins, a son and a daughter. The name Emain Macha, the Twins of Macha, comes from this. As she gave birth she screamed out that all who heard that scream would suffer from the same pangs for five days and four nights in their times of greatest difficulty. This affliction, ever afterward, seized all the men of Ulster who were there that day, and nine generations after them. Five days and four nights, or five nights and four days, the pangs lasted. For nine generations any Ulsterman in those pangs had no more strength than a woman on the bed of labour. Only three classes of people were free from the pangs of Ulster: the young boys of Ulster, the women, and Cúchulainn.

How the men of Ulster acquired their affliction is one of the many sub-plots in the famous *Táin Bó Cuailnge* (*The Cattle Raid of Cooley*). The *Táin* – described by Thomas Kinsella as 'the oldest vernacular epic in Western literature' – had a lively oral existence, surviving the vicissitudes of many centuries, before its different versions were written down. On one level it's pure adventure. On another it's a beady examination of men and women – both sexes equally regarded, equally imbued with wit and intelligence – when beset by folly and passion. They happen to be Celtic aristocrats, the cream of a remarkable race, but it's the ordinariness of their humanity, in spite of their importance in a now stern hierarchy, that so vividly gives them life. 'We Irish,' wrote W. B. Yeats in his preface to Lady Gregory's *Cuchulain of Muirthemne*, 'should keep these personages much in our hearts, for they lived in the places where we ride and go marketing, and sometimes they have met one another on the hills that cast their shadows upon our doors at evening. When I was a child I had only to climb the hill behind the house to see long, blue, ragged hills flowing along the southern horizon. What beauty was lost to me, what depth of emotion is still perhaps lacking in me, because nobody told me, not even the merchant captains who knew everything, that Cruachan of the Enchantments lay behind those long, blue, ragged hills!'

The *Táin* begins mildly. At Yeats's enchanted Cruachan pillow-talk was taking place. Medb, Queen of Connacht, and her consort, Ailill, were idly chatting in their royal bed. Never an easy woman, the Queen was yet again explaining to her husband how she couldn't have married a man less rich than

Tumulus of New Grange in the Boyne Valley, 3rd millenium BC. *As we look we feel in the presence of a lost world. We are out of touch. We have no bridge on which to step across so many centuries.* (*The Irish*: Sean O'Faolain)

16

she herself because he would have been shown up by her riches, or one less courageous because, embarrassingly, he might have turned away in battle, or a jealous man because there might yet be other men in her life. She was in a tetchy mood that night and before the conversation came to an end she had drawn up lists of her own possessions and Ailill's, just to make certain that he didn't have more. In fact he did. He had a hefty white-horned bull that couldn't be matched by any of hers.

It isn't difficult to imagine what the first listeners to this story must have imagined also: the spoilt, hasty Medb afterwards dwelling on all this silliness in her splendid abode, calling upon her druids for advice, walking alone with pet dogs, seeking signs in nature. Why should her husband, good and honourable though he was, possess more than she, since she was Queen in her own right? If Ailill outdid her in the matter would it not seem to the people of Connacht that it was he, the man, who mattered more?

Far away in the pastured North, near the hinterland of Carlingford Lough, there was a brown bull that was reputed to be as magnificent as Ailill's. From this might be bred other bulls, Medb reckoned, and so dispatched messengers with a request that she should be lent the animal for a year. She would pay its owner handsomely: fifty heifers or, if he should prefer it, an acreage in Connacht equal to his own in Ulster, a chariot worth twenty-one serving maids, and her own generous affection, the freedom of her friendly thighs.

It was a handsome offer and although the men of Ulster clearly would not be pleased to learn that a famous local bull was to be sent into the service of the Queen of Connacht, it so happened that the men of Ulster did not have the luxury of choices being still afflicted with the weakness of a woman in pregnancy. Because of this, the messengers from Connacht found the bull's owner only too eager to fall in with their propositions. Drinking belowstairs, however, they were undiplomatic enough to state the obvious: that if an agreement hadn't been reached the animal could very easily have been taken by force. Ulster's pride was outraged: the messengers returned without their prize, and the war for the Bull of Cuailnge (often spelt Cuailgne) began. So, too, did one of the most famous of all Irish journeys, the long trek north-east from Connacht, charted here by Thomas Kinsella:

> The Monday after Samain they set out. This is the way
> they went, southeast from Cruachan Ai:
>   through Muicc Cruinb,
>   through Terloch Teóra Crích, the marshy lake bed

Above: Skellig Michael, Co. Kerry.

Below: standing stones, Clounsharragh, Co. Kerry.

---

where three territories meet,
by Tuaim Móna, the peat ridge,
through Cúil Silinne, where Carrcin Lake is now – it
  was named after Silenn, daughter of Madchar,
by Fid and Bolga, woods and hills,
through Coltain, and across the Sinann river,
through Glúne Gabair,
over Trego Plain, of the spears,
through Tethba, North and South,
through Tiarthechta,
through Ord, 'the hammer,'
through Sláis southward,
by the river Indiuind, 'the anvil,'
through Carn,
through Ochtrach, 'the dung heap,'
through Midi, the land of Meath,
through Finnglassa Assail, of the clear streams,
by the river Deilt,
through Delind,
through Sailig,
through Slaibre of the herds,
through Slechta, where they hewed their way . . .

Obligingly, Ailill accompanied Medb as an ally. So did Fergus, he who had been King of Ulster until usurped by Conchubar, and since he knew the lie of this particular land better than anyone, Medb gave him the task of finding the best route. But as the army drew close to his own familiar landscape, Fergus felt homesick and guilty. He turned south again, trailing everyone behind him in a circle. Medb, who was occasionally inclined to reward Fergus with her generous affection, was less affectionate now.

'Fergus, there is something wrong.
What kind of road is this we're taking?
– straying to the south or north,
crossing every kind of land.

Ailill and his army
begin to think of treachery.
Or have you not yet set your mind
to leading us upon our way?

If old friendship is the cause
give up your first place on the march.
Perhaps another can be found
to take us on our proper way.'

Fergus answered:

'Medb, what is troubling you?
There's no treachery in this.
The land where I am taking you
– remember it is Ulster.

I take these turnings as they come
not to bring the host to harm
but to miss the mighty man
who protects Murtheimne Plain.

Do you think I don't know
every winding way I take?
I think ahead, trying to miss
Cúchulainn son of Sualdam.'

But Medb's soldiers must have been somewhat bewildered. Had Shakespeare ever discovered the story of the two bulls there would at this point have been a comic interlude, three or four military yokels scratching their heads over hills and trees that looked remarkably like the hills and trees of a week ago.

southward by Ochaine hill,
northward by Uatu,
by the river Dub,
southward through Comur,
through Tromma,
through Othromma eastward,
through Sláni and its pasture Gortsláni,
southward by Druim Licce, 'the flagstone ridge,'
by Ath Gabla, the ford of the forked branch,
through Ard Achad, the high field,
northward by Féraind,
by Finnabair,
through Assi southward,
by the ridge Druim Sálfinn,
by the ridge Druim Cain, on the Midluachair road,
by mac Dega's ridge,
by Eódond Mór and Eódond Bec, the great dark yew-tree and the lesser,
by Méthe Tog and Méthe nEoin, 'squirrel neck' and 'bird neck,'
by the ridge Druim Cáemtechta,
through Scúaip and Imscúaip,
through Cenn Ferna,
through Baile and Aile . . .

Through Meath and Louth the huge army hurried now, chariots and horses, druids, bards, poets, fools, satirists, and camp-followers. A spirit from Rath

Cruachan's otherworld – or Sidhe – had earlier warned Medb that all was not going to be well. Even though King Conchubar and the fighting men of Ulster were debilitated, this Sidhe shadow, in the borrowed shape of a beautiful young girl, spoke of blood and death, and destruction for Connacht and its allies. Medb was undeterred. On and on she urged her men, her obsession a passion now.

> through Báil Scena and Dáil Scena,
> through Fertse,
> by the wooded promontory Ros Lochad,
> through Sale,
> through Lochmach, or Muid Loga,
> through Anmag, the noble plain,
> by Dinn height,
> by the river Deilt,
> by the river Dubglais,
> through Fid Mór, or Fid Mórthruaille, the Wood of the Great Scabbard,
> to the river Colptha
> and to the river Cronn in Cuailnge.

But in her warning the Sidhe girl had spoken of the extraordinary Cúchulainn of Murtheimne, the only warrior in all the province of Ulster who continued to be spared the curse of Macha.

> The blood starts from warriors' wounds
> – total ruin – at his touch:
> your warriors dead, the warriors
> of Deda mac Sin prowling loose;
> torn corpses, women wailing,
> because of him – the Forge-Hound.

He was a stripling of modest size, a boy wonder who changed into divine form when he engaged in battle. And the prophecy from the Sidhe was no idle speculation: as Medb now discovered, Cúchulainn indeed stood between her and the rich grasslands of the North, and he alone seemed like being enough.

'Well,' Ailill said, 'let us be off.'
They went to Mag Muceda, the Pig-keeper's Plain, and there Cúchulainn cut down an oak tree in their path and cut an ogam message into its side. He wrote there that no one was to pass that oak, until a warrior had leaped it in his chariot at the first attempt. So they pitched their tents and set themselves to leaping the tree in their chariots. Thirty horses fell on that spot, and thirty chariots were smashed there, and the place has been called Belach nAne ever since, the Pass where they Drove.

Places, and their naming, feature prominently in the *Táin Bó Cuailnge*. When Medb's armies are finally driven from Ulster she succeeds at least in taking back

The River Shannon near Athlone, the town at the heart of Ireland, called
after the loins of a bull.

with her to Connacht the bull she came for, and there's a gory postscript. The
two bulls – Donn Cuailnge and Finnbennach – fight it out, Donn Cuailnge
achieving a narrow victory. With the remains of his adversary skewered on his
horns, he crashes about, scattering bones and liver and lights all over the lakes
and mountains, naming them as he goes. Thomas Kinsella translates again:

> The armies went to kill him, but Fergus stopped them and let him go anywhere he
> liked. He headed toward his own land. He stopped to drink in Finnlethe on the way.
> He left Finnbennach's shoulderblade there – from which comes Finnlethe, the
> White One's Shoulderblade, as the name of that district. He drank again at Ath
> Luain, and left Finnbennach's loins there – that is how the place was named Ath
> Luain, the Ford of the Loins. He uttered a bellow at Iraird Cuillenn that was heard
> through the whole province. He drank again at Tromma, where Finnbennach's
> liver fell from his two horns – from which comes the name Tromma, or liver. He

came to Etan Tairb and set his brow against the hill at Ath Da Ferta – from which comes the name Etan Tairb, the Bull's Brow, in Murtheimne Plain. Then he went by the Midluachair road to Cuib, where he had dwelt with the milkless cow of Dáire, and he tore up the ground there – from which comes the name Gort mBúraig, the Field of the Trench. Then he went on until he fell dead between Ulster and Uí Echach at Druim Tairb. So Druim Tairb, the Ridge of the Bull, is the name of that place.

In the cycle of Cúchulainn sagas, in which feats and marvels are strewn as thickly as the bodies, Cúchulainn himself, like Medb and Ailill and Fergus and so many of the others, emerges as a person as well as a magic-maker. One of the most moving episodes in the *Táin* concerns his relationship with his childhood friend, Ferdia, whom he is obliged to fight in the run of duty, whom he dreads having to kill and to whom he might even prefer to lose. Cúchulainn is a kind of Old Testament Christ, mystically born, a mixture of gentleness and extreme ferocity. As a boy he displayed extraordinary self-denial by taking the place of a blacksmith's watchdog which had been killed before it could attack him, and at that time of his life was rarely encountered unaccompanied by his hurling stick, with which he practised the game as he travelled the byways of Ulster. Generation after generation, his creators between them developed the Irish arch-hero: champion games-player, eyed everywhere by women, a quiet presence until circumstances rouse him. He belongs to the natural world from which so mysteriously he emerged, his spirit one with woods and valleys and riverbanks, his extra-earthly powers deriving from a flock of birds that ceremoniously arranged his birth.

The *Táin Bó Cuailnge*, long after its fiery spirit had evaporated in Ireland, was written down by Christian monks. Thomas Kinsella translates from the Irish of the *Book of the Dun Cow*, which was compiled in the monastery of Clonmacnoise in the twelfth century; and from the later *Yellow Book of Lecan*; and from the *Book of Leinster*. But the feeling of a told story, of the oral storyteller's art, colours the *Táin* from start to finish, as it does the several variations of another renowned, even more feverish, Irish journey, that of Diarmuid and Grainne. These illicit lovers, already defeated by chance and circumstance, flee through trackless forest-lands and bog, no town or village ever breaking the brown-green monotony. They are perpetually in danger from their pursuers, as animals are from hunters, and, like animals, they sleep fitfully, sharing with them the sounds of the night.

> The stag is not asleep in the east,
> he never ceases belling,
> although he is cosy in the blackbirds' wood,
> he has no mind for sleep.

Pleasant and lovely was the flight of birds and their song. There were nine
scores of birds with a silver chain between each couple. Each score went in its
own flight, nine flights altogether, and two birds out in front of each flight with
a yoke of silver between them. (The Táin: How Cúchulainn was Begotten.
Translated from the Irish by Thomas Kinsella)

Why is not the hornless doe asleep,
calling for her speckled calf?
Running over the tops of the bushes
she cannot sleep in her lair.

The linnct is awake and twittering
above the tips of the swaying trees:
they are all chattering in the woods –
and even the thrush is not asleep.

Why does not the wild duck sleep,
not sleep, nor drowse?
Why does it not sleep in its nest?
Why is it swimming steadily with all its strength?

To-night the grouse does not sleep
above the high, stormy, heathery hill;
sweet the cry of her clear throat,
sleepless among the streams.

from *The Flight of Diarmuid and Grainne*. Anonymous.
Translated from the Irish by Sean O'Faolain.

Individual Celts, men or women, must have created out of nothing the hard
grain around which each plot developed, to emerge eventually as fiction in
poetry or prose. The oral tradition of storytelling that followed this conception
is one that has thrived on decoration and variety, and the storyteller himself –
part actor, part originator – must have at an early stage acquired a precise rôle in
the ancient entertainment business. The better ones would presumably have
added whole new conceptions and characters to the saga-lore, one cycle
begetting the next. For the lesser luminaries a skilful theatrical presence was
perhaps enough to get by with. All of them would have been amateurs in the
first place, part-time traders in anecdote, myth and history. But professional-
ism, and with it an honoured and vital place in the Celtic scheme of life, would
over long generations have drawn the storyteller to the edge of society, making
him both special and an outsider. And while further battles were waged and
territory rearranged after victory and defeat, the storytellers attached to this
court or that must often have found themselves patronless and forgotten. Like
the early food-seekers searching an unknown landscape for anything it offered,
like the fated Diarmuid and Grainne, travel was what they came to understand,
arriving out of nowhere to recount the remarkable deeds of remarkable people.
Such itinerant life is a familiar Irish phenomenon, and those lost tale-bearers –
whenever it was they first appeared – were the beginning of a convention that
was to last for two thousand or so years in Ireland. Nor does it seem fanciful to
suggest that, pausing between sagas, the storytellers also carried tidings of
current affairs, broadcasting the news as well as their turbulent historical
fictions.

Certainly there was news to be imparted. As Roman strength waned in
Britain, some of the Irish had moved into Wales and Cornwall and Scotland,
bringing with them their ogham inscriptions and the Irish language. They gave
Scotland its name, and ensured that these three regions of Britain remained, and
continued to remain, outside the social and cultural mainstream. Today the
Celtic fringe of that other island could not be more different from the modern
state of Ireland, but it does share with it a temperament and a sensibility. And,
by chance, there is a similarity of landscape and architecture: the grandeur of
Wales and Scotland occasionally resembles Ireland's, and to find an English
town with a provincial flavour that is reminiscent of such towns in Ireland you
look in the West Country: remove the swinging Lloyd's Bank sign and the inn

signs from the little towns of the moors and for an eerie moment or two you might be in Tullow or Killorglin.

But the similarities are skin-deep, and the wonder really is that Ireland is so different. Its appearance is unrelated to England's because, to start with, the Romans decided not to extend their empire beyond the Irish Sea and because, centuries later, it did not receive the grimy face-lift of the Industrial Revolution. Yet the Romans did, in another sense, spread an indelible influence over the island they never bothered with. After one of the Irish forays into the West of Britain a youth was carried back to Ireland and into slavery: Patricius, son of Capurnius, was inordinately proud of his Roman citizenship, his Latin and his Christianity. Affected by the land he found himself in, he determined to bring to it the language, the ways, and the religion of the Romans. He tended sheep on the mountainside of Slemish in Co. Antrim, escaped, returned to Britain and made his way to Gaul. According to his own account, he was consecrated in 432 by the Church of Gaul, requested to return to the place of his captivity and entrusted with the task of converting its untutored people. After which, everything in Ireland was different.

Slemish, Co. Antrim. Pope Celestine I had already sent Ireland her first bishop, Palladius. Little is known of him and it was left to Patrick in his mountain loneliness to envisage, for the first time, an Ireland of saints and scholars. Songs and stories had no longer to rely on word-of-mouth existence. With Christianity, literature began.

The Gentle Years

I arise to-day
Through the strength of heaven:
Light of sun,
Radiance of moon,
Splendour of fire,
Speed of lightning,
Swiftness of wind,
Depth of sea,
Stability of earth,
Firmness of rock.
from *The Deer's Cry*, also known as *Patrick's Breastplate*.
Translated from an anonymous source (though sometimes attributed to St
Patrick) by Kuno Meyer.

BUILD THOU a monastery, St Patrick is said to have abjured St Kieran, inaugurating the Holy Ireland which, with some unholy variation, has been with us ever since. High crosses replaced standing stones and ogham stones, and for a time at least protective walls gave way to cloisters. You cannot today pass through the Irish landscape without experiencing in the presence of those great crosses the same awe which, centuries before their erection, the Celts themselves must have felt as they gazed upon the graves of their predecessors. You cannot look upon the illustrated gospels of the *Book of Kells* or the *Book of Durrow* without feeling that that extraordinary art has become as much part of the Irish scenic backdrop as the mountains of Connemara or the Cliffs of Moher. The ultimate magnificence of Celtic influence in Ireland, a unique conjunction of people and place, was reached when the story of Christ stole the limelight from Cúchulainn.

The convolutions of ancient myth, the honeycomb of anecdote nestling within the major plot, the layers of fresh invention: all of it, when it was at last recorded, created an effect not unlike the elaborations of the decorated gospels. And the chronicling ecclesiastics, though meticulous in their conservation, added something of their own whether they wished to or not, a certain style, a certain way of putting things. As well, they often protested at what must occasionally have seemed to them to be pagan nonsense – the exploits of the wily Morrígan, one of the three goddesses of battle, for ever seeking to outdo the orderly Dagdá, the wild exaggeration of human capability, so very different from the Christ's truth that guided monastic life. As decades and then centuries

High Cross, Kells, Co. Meath.

went by, these dutiful recorders may have found themselves preferring the spirit of the poetry which their task was to preserve also. Translated by Frank O'Connor, here is *The Hermit's Song*, inevitably anonymous and of no agreed date:

A hiding tuft, a green-barked yew-tree
  Is my roof,
While nearby a great oak keeps me
  Tempest-proof.

I can pick my fruit from an apple
  Like an inn,
Or can fill my fist where hazels
  Shut me in.

A clear well beside me offers
  Best of drink,
And there grows a bed of cresses
  Near its brink.

Pigs and goats, the friendliest neighbours,
  Nestle near,
Wild swine come, or broods of badgers,
  Grazing deer.

All the gentry of the county
  Come to call!
And the foxes come behind them,
  Best of all.

To what meals the woods invite me
  All about!
There are water, herbs and cresses,
  Salmon, trout.

A clutch of eggs, sweet mast and honey
  Are my meat,
Heathberries and whortleberries
  For a sweet.

All that one could ask for comfort
  Round me grows,
There are hips and haws and strawberries,
  Nuts and sloes.

And when summer spreads its mantle
  What a sight!
Marjoram and leeks and pignuts,
  Juicy, bright.

The asceticism of the early Irish church can still be sensed among the remains of the beehive habitations of monks on Skellig Michael, off the coast of Kerry.

Dainty redbreasts briskly forage
    Every bush,
Round and round my hut there flutter
    Swallow, thrush.

Bees and beetles, music-makers,
    Croon and strum;
Geese pass over, duck in autumn,
    Dark streams hum.

Angry wren, officious linnet
    And black-cap,
All industrious, and the woodpecker's
    Sturdy tap.

From the sea the gulls and herons
    Flutter in,
While in upland heather rises
    The grey hen.

In the year's most brilliant weather
    Heifers low
Through green fields, not driven nor beaten,
    Tranquil, slow.

In wreathed boughs the wind is whispering,
    Skies are blue,
Swans call, river water falling
    Is calling too.

It is a good deal easier to imagine such patient Christian scribes than it is the stone-age architects of the Boyne Valley burial places. Yet those distant people, possessed of an inspired imagination as their edifices so impressively indicate, must surely have known an unwritten literature as rich as the Celts'. Like the people themselves, it is a blank in the modern mind, just as the Celtic storyteller – in spite of the accessibility of the epics that gave him his *raison d'être* – remains hidden in the murkiness of time. As if acutely sensitive to these vacuums, the literate monk saw to it that he himself did not become elusive in the same way. As well as everything else, he chronicled his own garden world:

A hedge before me, one behind,
a blackbird sings from that,
above my small book many-lined
I apprehend his chat.

Up trees, in costumes buff,
mild accurate cuckoos bleat,
Lord love me, good the stuff
I write in a shady seat.
Anonymous. Translated from the Irish by Flann O'Brien.

Early Gaelic poetry has a vividness of imagery accompanied often by unusual rhythm, but it is perhaps more notable for a simplicity that is in stark contrast to the swagger of the myths: for the second time in Ireland a rumbustious Celtic vigour has calmed. Even so, the pastoral tapestry that this period registers is not without its thorns. *Patrick, you chatter too loud*, protests Oisín, son of Fionn, in a poem that has its roots in the eighth century. *You lift your crozier too high*. Oisín, spirited away to the Land of Youth in the heyday of the heroic age, returns to find a cloistered Ireland a-jabber with masses: he is not impressed. And Mad Sweeney, a small-time king whom St Ronan turned into a bird, is a recurring figure in the poetry of the time, repeatedly voicing a preference – perhaps naturally in the circumstances – for the birdsong of the River Bann over the chime of churchbells. Sweeney, like Oisín, remains tied to, even possessed by, nature, 'the enemy', in Seamus Heaney's words, 'and the captive of the monastic tradition'. In translation, Heaney recaptures the mad king's noisy protest in 'one of Sweeney's frequent outbursts where his imagination is beautifully entangled with the vegetation and the weathers and animals of the countryside, [which] will have to stand for scores of similar poems from the sixth to the sixteenth century, all of them attesting to the god in the tree as a source of poetic inspiration.'

The bushy leafy oaktree
is highest in the wood,
the forking shoots of hazel
hide sweet hazel-nuts.

The alder is my darling,
all thornless in the gap,
some milk of human kindness
coursing in its sap.

The blackthorn is a jaggy creel
stippled with dark sloes;
green watercress is thatch on wells
where the drinking blackbird goes.

Sweetest of the leafy stalks,
the vetches strew the pathway;
the oyster-grass is my delight,
and the wild strawberry.

Low-set clumps of apple trees
drum down fruit when shaken;
scarlet berries clot like blood
on mountain rowan.

Briars curl in sideways,
arch a stickle back,
draw blood and curl up innocent
to sneak the next attack.

The yew tree in each churchyard
wraps night in its dark hood.
Ivy is a shadowy
genius of the wood.

Holly rears its windbreak,
a door in winter's face;
life-blood on a spear-shaft
darkens the grain of ash.

Birch tree, smooth and blessed,
delicious to the breeze,
high twigs plait and crown it
the queen of trees.

The aspen pales
and whispers, hesitates:
a thousand frightened scuts
race in its leaves.

But what disturbs me most
in the leafy wood
is the to and fro and to and fro
of an oak rod.

Anonymous. Translated from the Irish by Seamus Heaney.

But idylls – whether Christian or pagan – do not last long in the countryside, and the farmer has less time than the poet to consider the case of Oisín *versus* Patrick. He takes what he can get in the way of spiritual aid, and will pray as advised. In a plain life the seasons dictate, and whatever god there is is welcome as an intercessor. With no god at all the plainness is too much.

Here's my story; the stag cries,
Winter snarls as summer dies.

The wind bullies the low sun
In poor light; the seas moan.

Shapeless bracken is turning red,
The wildgoose raises its desperate head.

Birds' wings freeze where fields are hoary.
The world is ice. That's my story.

My Story. Anonymous.
Translated from the Irish by Brendan Kennelly.

Winter snarled even more menacingly for the people of the coast. The same sea which had risen at the time of the melting of the ice to give Ireland its island character continued to endow it with jagged beauty, and the fickle waves were rarely less than master: luck was necessary, prayers were said, when the people ventured out with boats. But the sea was an inspiration also.

Tempest on the plain of Lir
Bursts its barriers far and near,
And upon the rising tide
Wind and noisy winter ride –
Winter throws a shining spear.

A good season for staying is autumn; there is work then for everyone before
the very short days. . . .
In the black season of deep winter a storm of waves is roused along the
expanse of the world. . . .
Raw and cold is icy spring, cold will arise in the wind. . . .
A good season is summer for long journeys; quiet is the tall fire wood, which
the whistle of the wind will not stir. . . .
(*The Four Seasons*: Anonymous, 11th century. Translated from the Irish by
Kenneth Hurlstone Jackson)

When the wind blows from the east
All the billows seem possessed,
   To the west they storm away
   To the farthest, wildest bay
Where the light turns to its rest.

When the wind is from the north
The fierce and shadowy waves go forth,
   Leaping, snarling at the sky,
   To the southern world they fly
And the confines of the earth.

When the wind is from the west
All the waves that cannot rest
   To the east must thunder on
   Where the bright tree of the sun
Is rooted in the ocean's breast.

When the wind is from the south
The waves turn to a devil's broth,
   Crash in foam on Skiddy's beach,
   For Caladnet's summit reach,
Batter Limerick's grey-green mouth.

Ocean's full! The sea's in flood,
Beautiful is the ships' abode;
   In the Bay of the Two Beasts
   The sandy wind in eddies twists,
The rudder holds a shifting road.

Every bay in Ireland booms
When the flood against it comes –
   Winter throws a spear of fire!
   Round Scotland's shores and by Cantyre
A mountainous surging chaos glooms.

God's Son of hosts that none can tell
The fury of the storm repel!
   Dread Lord of the sacrament,
   Save me from the wind's intent,
Spare me from the blast of Hell.

                    Storm at Sea. Anonymous.
           Translated from the Irish by Frank O'Connor.

Tempestuous sea, Dingle Peninsula, Co. Kerry.

Tory Island and Gola, Inishmurray and Inishkea, Achill and Aran and the Blaskets, Mutton Island and the Maidens: these are the offspring of such seas, which in a quieter mood have given *The Old Woman of Beare* a scummy surface to see herself reflected in. Her story, also, can be attributed to nobody; the translator is Brendan Kennelly.

The sea crawls from the shore
Leaving there
The despicable weed,
A corpse's hair.
In me,
The desolate withdrawing sea.

The Old Woman of Beare am I
Who once was beautiful.
Now all I know is how to die.
I'll do it well.

Look at my skin
Stretched tight on the bone.
Where kings have pressed their lips,
The pain, the pain.

I don't hate the men
Who swore the truth was in their lies.
One thing alone I hate –
Women's eyes.

The young sun
Gives its youth to everyone,
Touching everything with gold.
In me, the cold.

The cold. Yet still a seed
Burns there.
Women love only money now.
But when
I loved, I loved
Young men.

Young men whose horses galloped
On many an open plain
Beating lightning from the ground.
I loved such men.

And still the sea
Rears and plunges into me,

Shoving, rolling through my head
Images of the drifting dead.

A soldier cries
Pitifully about his plight;
A king fades
Into the shivering night.

Does not every season prove
That the acorn hits the ground?
Have I not known enough of love
To know it's lost as soon as found?

I drank my fill of wine with kings,
Their eyes fixed on my hair.
Now among the stinking hags
I chew the cud of prayer.

Time was the sea
Brought kings as slaves to me.
Now I near the face of God
And the crab crawls through my blood.

I loved the wine
That thrilled me to my fingertips;
Now the mean wind
Stitches salt into my lips.

The coward sea
Slouches away from me.
Fear brings back the tide
That made me stretch at the side
Of him who'd take me briefly for his bride.

The sea grows smaller, smaller now.
Farther, farther it goes
Leaving me here where the foam dries
On the deserted land,
Dry as my shrunken thighs,
As the tongue that presses my lips,
As the veins that break through my hands.

The sea carried the unshakable faith of Irish monks to Europe, where their presence drew attention to the island they left behind. Did they in their cowled innocence speak of it as it is so enticingly described in John Montague's lines from the *Book of Invasions*? Did their nostalgia sound like an invitation?

Fertile fruitful mountains,
Fruitful moist woods,

Moist overflowing lochs,
Flowing hillside springs . . .

They may even have gone one better and proudly mentioned ornaments in gold and silver, a holy magnificence in abbeys and churches that was a sight to behold. However it was, that same sea carried back the Vikings. Up estuaries and rivers they sailed, to pillage and to conquer – and later to contribute hugely to the Irish world. They altered its geography with towns such as Wexford, Cork, Waterford, Dublin itself; and it is likely that the round tower, designed with sanctuary in mind and destined to become so distinctive a feature in Irish landscape, first came into being during the Viking years. The Viking presence is treasured in Ireland today, but in its time it was no joke. Only when there was 'wild upheaval' in the sea, a contemporary poet noted, could the people of the coasts and rivers sleep easily in their beds.

Due principally to the efforts of Malachy, King of Meath, and Brian Boru, King of Munster, peace was eventually restored in Ireland – but not before history had become so dramatic and outrageous that the Celts at their most imaginative are instantly recalled. An astute Viking – Olaf of the Sandals, who ruled the kingdom of Dublin – was defeated by Malachy and retired to Iona, where he later died a Christian. He left behind a queen called Gormflath, another of those fateful women who have played star parts in Irish history.

The 5th-century monk, Brendan of Clonfert, and his companions, who, on one of the most famous of sea voyages, landed their boat on top of a whale thinking it to be an island.

Round tower at water's edge, Devenish Isle, Lough Erne, Co. Fermanagh.

Affected by her beauty and her presence, Malachy married this sharp-witted widow but quickly abandoned her; then Brian Boru took her on, only to abandon her in turn. Not unnaturally miffed by the repetitious nature of this treatment, Gormflath prevailed upon her son, Sitric, and her brother, Maelmora, to seek overseas aid in order to overthrow the now elderly Malachy and Brian. Sigurd the Stout, earl of Orkney, entered the plot: all Ireland, and Gormflath herself, were to be his if he arrived with a suitable army. In the conflict which followed, both he and Brian were slain. Wisely, Gormflath slipped away.

But this famous battle, at Clontarf near Dublin in 1014, was the end of the Viking terror. Brian Boru, a most civilized king, had restored the dignity of the Church and managed to breathe life into a culture that had shown signs of withering. And what he began in his lifetime continued for long after his death. His patronage and encouragement had brought about a revival of the craftsmanship in precious metals which had been so distinguished in the past.

Cormac's Chapel on the Rock of Cashel, which had long been the seat of
Irish kings, pre-dates the Norman invasion, being completed in 1134.

Poetry and epics had been gathered in. An Irish Romanesque style developed
in architecture, to be further enriched by the French influence of the Cistercians
when they arrived in 1142. By the end of the twelfth century ancient Ireland
was complete.

But also by the end of the twelfth century the Normans had arrived.
Bustling and inquisitive, they came from Wales and England, prospectors with
an eye for land, no more than a handful when first they insinuated themselves.
Spreading about them their enterprise and skill, they cleverly attached
themselves to Irish allies. Before they called for reinforcements they built their
castles and their roads, and slipped into the seaside towns of the Vikings. They
shared a religion but not a language with the natives whose skyline they quite
dramatically altered. Christ Church Cathedral in Dublin was founded by them
towards the end of the twelfth century, and as late as the fifteenth, Holy Cross
Abbey near Thurles was rebuilt by its Cistercian monks in the Norman style.

Holy Cross Abbey, on the River Suir, near Thurles in Co. Tipperary.

For generations it had housed a fragment of the True Cross, and had been endowed with a generous acreage of land 'in honour of the Almighty God and Holy Mary, the Virgin, and St Benedict and the Holy Cross'.

In politics and culture, in the Norman manner of doing things, the foundations were laid of what was to be for many centuries England's Ireland. Ireland's own acquisitive ambitions – that Celtic tiresomeness in Western Britain – belonged by this time to the past, and was probably not even known about by the thrusting young barons who were giving the Irish a dose of their ancestors' medicine. The barons would have moved in anyway: two islands so closely placed invite such traffic, and coveting the possessions of a neighbour was hardly, for the man of the Middle Ages, the most heinous sin.

But having made their purpose clear, the Normans performed constructively. They did indeed become more Irish than the Irish, and Norman names today – Fitzgerald, Lacy, Butler, Burke, Joyce – are as much part of Ireland as Ryan or MacCarthy. They were assimilated, they contributed enormously. Just as the fortunes of the locals waxed and waned so did their own, for not all the Normans, by any means, remained within the ruling class. Travelling in Ireland many centuries after their advent, George Borrow noticed the prevalence of ruined castles, ' . . . so thick and numerous that the face of the country appears studded with them'. These, with churches and abbeys that are quite unlike the Christian modesty of the previous few centuries, are the Norman contribution to the countenance of Ireland. Cashel, in Co. Tipperary, which the first King of Munster chose for his capital, flowered beneath a subtlety that was more European than local. Crosses and carved figures acquired or reflected a style that was also foreign. Interestingly, such developments often arrived ahead of the Normans themselves, fashion anticipating its most enthusiastic conveyor. Cormac's Chapel on the Rock of Cashel was finished in 1134; it wasn't until 1170 that Strongbow was helped on his way into Leinster by Dermot MacMurrough, its king. If that historic welcome had not occurred, there is little doubt that Norman influence, with or without the bloodshed, would have continued to drift into Ireland. The barons added fuss and emphasis to it, and they hurried matters up.

The 'triumphant clamour of great Clonmacnoise', the monastery world described by the poet Oengus in 800, seems now to belong to a fading age. Translating from the Irish of Angus O'Gillan, T. W. Rolleston later caught the whisper of the bustling monastery's ghosts, famous figures dominating the place's humbler dead:

> In a quiet water'd land, a land of roses,
>   Stands Saint Kieran's city fair;
> And the warriors of Erin in their famous generations
>   Slumber there.

Clonmacnoise, Co. Offaly.

There beneath the dewy hillside sleep the noblest
  Of the clan of Conn,
Each below his stone with name in branching Ogham
  And the sacred knot thereon.

There they laid to rest the seven Kings of Tara,
  There the sons of Cairbrè sleep –
Battle-banners of the Gael that in Kieran's plain of crosses
  Now their final hosting keep.

And in Clonmacnoise they laid the men of Teffia,
  And right many a lord of Breagh;
Deep the sod above Clan Creidè and Clan Conaill,
  Kind in hall and fierce in fray.

Many and many a son of Conn the Hundred-fighter
  In the red earth lies at rest;
Many a blue eye of Clan Colman the turf covers,
  Many a swan-white breast.

Clonmacnoise.

The dedicated existence of the monks who wrote down the *Táin Bó Cuailnge*, the simplicity of *The Hermit's Song*, the leisurely countryside in which only the elements were the enemy: all that, while not shattered, was certainly shaken by Norman intrusion. Busy, businesslike French was added, as the new language of the court, to Irish and ecclesiastical Latin, and the independent ways of the old Irish Church were more noticeable than they had been. It was, to some degree, to counter this isolation within European Christianity that the Cistercian and Augustinian abbeys were founded both before and after the Norman invasion. The whole period was one of transformation, the end of the conservative spirit that had so lovingly garnered and polished all that had come its way. With a speed not known before, a different Ireland was being created whether the natives liked it or not, an Ireland with a sense of politics and even of the urban life that was to come. It was then that the Irish learnt to conform, and the lesson was not wholly painless, for they had been – in marked contrast to their reputation since – the least adaptable of people.

The nineteenth-century poet James Clarence Mangan looked back to this time of upheaval, imbuing the manners and landscape of the West of Ireland with a spirit which progress had passed by. Norman techniques are certainly to be found in what remains of the friaries of Connacht, but the old order otherwise persisted and there is more than a little documentary truth in Mangan's vision. Ireland's poorest and most beautiful province has always had a way of holding foreign sophistication at bay, by chance or by the very nature of its being.

Trim Castle, Co. Meath, begun by Hugh de Lacy in 1172, was completed in 1220.

I walked entranced
    Through a land of Morn;
The sun, with wondrous excess of light,
    Shone down and glanced
        Over seas of corn
And lustrous gardens aleft and right.
    Even in the clime
        Of resplendent Spain,
Beams no such sun upon such a land;
    But it was the time,
        'Twas in the reign,
Of Cáhal Mór of the Wine-red Hand.

    Anon stood nigh
        By my side a man
Of princely aspect and port sublime.
    Him queried I –
        'O, my Lord and Khan,
What clime is this, and what golden time?'

47

When he – 'The clime
    Is a clime to praise,
The clime is Erin's, the green and bland;
    And it is the time,
    These be the years,
Of Cáhal Mór of the Wine-red Hand!'

Then saw I thrones,
    And circling fires,
And a Dome rose near me, as by a spell,
    Whence flowed the tones
    Of silver lyres,
And many voices in wreathed swell;
    And their thrilling chime
    Fell on mine ears
As the heavenly hymn of an angel-band –
    'It is now the time,
    These be the years,
Of Cáhal Mór of the Wine-red Hand!'

I sought the hall,
    And, behold! – a change
From light to darkness, from joy to woe!
    King, nobles, all,
    Looked aghast and strange;
The minstrel-group sate in dumbest show!
    Had some great crime
    Wrought this dread amaze,
This terror? None seemed to understand
    'Twas then the time
    We were in the days,
Of Cáhal Mór of the Wine-red Hand.

I again walked forth,
    But lo! the sky
Showed fleckt with blood, and an alien sun
    Glared from the north,
    And there stood on high,
Amid his shorn beams, a skeleton!
    It was by the stream
    Of the castled Maine,
One Autumn eve, in the Teuton's land,
    That I dreamed this dream
    Of the time and reign
Of Cáhal Mór of the Wine-red Hand!

A Vision of Connacht in the Thirteenth Century. James Clarence Mangan (1803–49).

Irish Romanesque survives Norman sophistication at Clonfert Cathedral,
Co. Galway, where the Celtic head cult is a continuing influence.

Croagh Patrick, Ireland's holiest mountain.

England's Ireland:
The Anglo-Irish World

ANY SURVEY of Irish or Anglo-Irish literature since 1170 becomes, sooner or later, ensnared with political complications. In Ireland you can escape neither politics nor history, for when you travel through the country today the long conflict its landscape has known does not as readily belong in the faraway past as Hastings or Stamford Bridge does for the English. The arrival of the Welsh Normans was the beginning of the 'eight centuries' so well remembered by later generations of disgruntled Irish, those years of conquest and colonization during which the Normans lost their identity and were replaced by the adventuring Tudors and by bickering Stuarts keen to make use of handy Irish armies. The forester's craft of clearing and replanting was applied to people; and Cromwell's puritanism was further purified in Irish bloodbaths that stimulated his crusading spirit. The attempted extinction of a language and a religion failed; famine mopped up the residue of yet more war. But the Normans, in becoming Irish, really did live up to the implications of that choice. One of them, Gerald Nugent, writing in Gaelic in the sixteenth century, clearly belonged in the island his forbears had found to their liking.

> Shore of fine fruit-bended trees,
> Shore of green grass-covered leas;
> Old plain of Ir, soft, showery,
> Wheatful, fruitful, fair, flow'ry.
>
> Home of priest and gallant knight
> Isle of gold-haired maidens bright
> Banba of the clear blue wave
> Of bold hearts and heroes brave.

> Translator unknown.

The Reformation was a stumbling-block. The Irish had marvelled as enthusiastically over the story of Christ as they had over that of Cúchulainn or Deirdre of the Sorrows. They had made a hero of St Patrick, and the need to believe, to accept with pleasurable awe the mysterious and the wonderful, had been part of their culture since first they revered the ghosts of their predecessors. Snatching their religion from them cut more deeply even than snatching their land: they felt it as an attempt to purloin their very soul. This Irish instinct for the mystery of faith, for the supernatural, for the excitement of yet another complex epic, had become an infectious part of the national make-up: among both Catholics and Protestants there is still an urgency about religion that is not to be found among the people of the richer and more powerful neighbouring island. Faith and ordinary life, faith and disaster, faith and nature: in Irishness all belong together. Faith has made Croagh Patrick a holy mountain and Lough Derg a holy lake, and the village of Knock in Co. Mayo – where the Virgin was dramatically sighted on the evening of 21 August 1879, the eve of the Octave of the Assumption – an international rendezvous for pilgrims.

> I hear the stag's belling
>   Over the valley's steepness
> No music on earth
>   Can move me like its sweetness.
>
> Christ, Christ, hear me!
>   Christ, Christ of Thy meekness!
> Christ, Christ, love me!
>   Sever me not from Thy sweetness!
>   from *The Sweetness of Nature*. Anonymous.
>   Translated from the Irish by Frank O'Connor.

Myrtle Grove, where Sir Walter Ralegh – who was Mayor of Youghal – was visited by Edmund Spenser.

Faire harbour that them seems; so in they entred arre. (*The Faerie Queene*: Edmund Spenser)

But if faith trailed trouble in its wake, there were also compensations. At a time when the country was still reeling from the excesses of the English Reformation, Sir Walter Ralegh planted on his estates in Co. Cork what was to become Ireland's primary source of nourishment, the potato. Sir Walter had been given 40,000 acres, but he and his West Country squires were as unpopular with Munster's 'Old English' – the descendants of the Norman families – as they were with the Irish. Ralegh's house is still a tourist sight, next to the beautiful St Mary's Church in the seaside town of Youghal. There is a somewhat dubious claim that Shakespeare acted in this pleasant watering place at the mouth of the Blackwater, but there's no doubt about the presence of Edmund Spenser within riding distance of its beaches and its walled grandeur. Spenser's Tower is hardly a landmark any more, though his voice at its most eloquent still speaks from the Blackwater countryside he loved. His naming of the trees recalls poor Mad Sweeney, even if it's extremely unlikely that Spenser ever heard of that distressful king.

53

Enforst to seeke some couert nigh at hand,
   A shadie groue not far away they spide,
   That promist ayde the tempest to withstand:
   Whose loftie trees yclad with sommers pride,
   Did spred so broad, that heauens light did hide,
   Not perceable with power of any starre:
   And all within were pathes and alleies wide,
   With footing worne, and leading inward farre:
Faire harbour that them seemes; so in they entred arre.

And foorth they passe, with pleasure forward led,
   Joying to heare the birdes sweete harmony,
   Which therein shrouded from the tempest dred,
   Seemd in their song to scorne the cruell sky.
   Much can they prayse the trees so straight and hy,
   The sayling Pine, the Cedar proud and tall,
   The vine-prop Elme, the Poplar neuer dry,
   The builder Oake, sole king of forrests all,
The Aspine good for staues, the Cypresse funerall.

The Laurell, meed of mightie Conquerours
   And Poets sage, the Firre that weepeth still,
   The Willow worne of forlorne Paramours,
   The Eugh obedient to the benders will,
   The Birch for shaftes, the Sallow for the mill,
   The Mirrhe sweete bleeding in the bitter wound,
   The warlike Beech, the Ash for nothing ill,
   The fruitful Oliue, and the Platane round,
The caruer Holme, the Maple seeldom inward sound.

Led with delight, they thus beguile the way,
   Vntill the blustring storme is ouerblowne;
   When weening to returne, whence they did stray,
   They cannot finde that path, which first was showne,
   But wander too and fro in wayes vnknowne,
   Furthest from end then, when they neerest weene,
   That makes them doubt, their wits be not their owne:
   So many pathes, so many turnings seene,
That which of them to take, in diuerse doubt they been.

from *The Faerie Queene* (I. i. st. 7, 8, 9, 10).

Spenser lived near the village of Doneraile, which was part of a 3,000-acre estate granted to him in 1586. He had been Clerk of the Court of Chancery in Dublin, a civil servant well rewarded for his loyalty. *The Faerie Queene* must have been written in part at Doneraile; certainly *Colin Clouts come home againe* was. The lush Co. Cork landscape around the stronghold of Kilcolman,

The remains of Kilcolman Castle, Spenser's Tower, attacked and burned by insurgents in 1598 and today almost lost in the surrounding landscape.

granted to him also, is the landscape that comes most naturally to mind when reading Spenser – lush because so often the day is 'suddeine ouercast', clouds heralding in the familiar Irish manner the 'hideous storme of raine'.

The Anglo-Irish aristocracy, constantly fed and rejuvenated by fresh arrivals from England, thrived particularly well in Co. Cork. The Earl of Desmond, of the Norman–Welsh family of Geraldines, had recognized in 1562 the sovereignty of Queen Elizabeth and his own feudal position beneath it. He had also agreed to prosecute all poets who 'in their ditties and rhymes' did not toe the royal line. But this conciliatory co-operation on the part of the new Irish – or old English – didn't last long. Rebellion was on the way, and by 1586 Elizabeth had attained the Desmond lands. More than 21,000 acres were planted with fresh settlers from England, but Munster absorbed them rather better than might have been expected, with the result that they in turn came to feel themselves one with the established gentry.

The great houses and demesnes followed at their own pace, their social life flourishing within a graceful world that anticipated the eighteenth century. Enlivened by the edginess of mixed loyalties, it was a world always capable of finding answers to its innate problems, of smoothing without apparent effort what should have been a perpetually ruffled surface. Out of its good manners and its style was eventually to emerge a considerable literature, and already it was establishing a landscape of its own: a succession of what were then highly individual gardens with a special local flavour. As experts on landscaping in the Elizabethan period have pointed out, *The Faerie Queene* describes in passing this novel scenery – man-made effects side by side with what nature provided, a rare mixture in England at that time, but increasingly fashionable in Ireland:

> There the most daintie Paradise on ground,
>   It selfe doth offer to his sober eye,
>   In which all pleasures plenteously abound,
>   And none does others happinesse enuye:
>   The painted flowres, the trees upshooting hye,
>   The dales for shade, the hilles for breathing space,
>   The trembling groves, the Christall running by;
>   And that, which all faire workes doth most aggrace,
> The art, which all that wrought, appeared in no place.

> One would have thought, (so cunningly, the rude,
>   And scorned parts were mingled with the fine,)
>   That nature had for wantonesse ensude
>   Art, and that Art at Nature did repine;
>   So striving each th'other to undermine,
>   Each did the others worke more beautifie;
>   So diff'ring both in willes, agreed in fine:
>   So all agreed through sweete diversitie
> This Gardin to adorne with all varitie.

(II. xii. st. 48, 49)

More than a hundred years went by without much apparent change in the Irish landowner's vision of how a garden should be. In 1737 Lord Orrery wrote to an English friend of 'a great Difference in the Complexion of the two Islands. Nature has been profusely beneficent to *Ireland*, and Art has been as much so to *England*. Here, we are beholden to nothing but the Creation; there, you are indebted to extensive Gardeners and costly Architects.'

And more than two centuries later The Knight of Glin and Edward Malins, who have contributed so much to our understanding of what early Irish gardens must have been like, agree that 'this is indeed the prime difference in landscaping in the two countries: Ireland was little tamed by art as the milder climate and higher rainfall produced profuse horticultural growth. In addition, the much indented coastline, the many natural loughs amid mountainous scenery provided material for landscaping which was readily incorporated.

Vernon Mount, Co. Cork. From the oil painting by Nathaniel Grogan, 1807.

These prospects, in which water played so large a part, created a very special harmony, unique to Ireland.'

'Remember,' wrote Lord Molesworth to his wife in 1709, 'to leave rounds or ovals. . . . The walks must be very narrow and close, yet the principal ones a little broader than the others.'

Jonathan Swift rode on the Molesworth estate near Swords, Co. Dublin, and would almost certainly have had a hand in planning the gardens. He had, in 1699, based his own gardens at Laracor, Co. Meath, on Moor Park in Surrey. Gardens fascinated him as much as they did his friend Alexander Pope, and it was their joint enthusiasm that brought many of the new landscaping ideas to Ireland. As soon as Swift became Dean of St Patrick's Cathedral in Dublin he set about arranging a larger garden than the modest one attached to the Deanery. For this purpose he leased part of the Liberties of St Patrick's and spent a very great deal of money on enclosing an area which he called Naboth's Vineyard. He successfully grew peaches and nectarines on a south-facing wall which he had specially lined with bricks in order to retain the sun's heat. He planted many elms in the churchyard, removing remains and tombstones in order to create the patterns he desired. Naboth's Vineyard had a little stream running through it and, as designed by Swift, was in no way formal. Of it, and of himself, he wrote:

> He'd treat with nothing that was Rare,
> But winding Walks and purer Air;
> Wou'd entertain without Expence,
> Or Pride, or vain Magnificence . . .
>
> from *An Apology to the Lady C-R-T*.

Naboth's Garden, on which the Meath Hospital now stands, was a rectangular strip of about one and a quarter acres. Paths wandered through shrubs and roses, willows grew along the stream; but none of it was grand enough for Swift, who devoted the excess of his horticultural energies to working with his friend, the Reverend Patrick Delany, on the Delville estate at Glasnevin, now a suburb of Dublin. The two got on well – something which could not always be counted upon where the Dean was concerned – and Delany's Delville became for Swift a treasure and an obsession. Unlike Naboth's Vineyard, it was already mature: orange trees grew in a parterre, a more impressive stream than the one at the Deanery tumbled prettily over rocks, the winding paths passed through glades and even a cave; deer and cattle added a flavour of the more mundane landscape from which the estate had been created.

The eighteenth-century modern garden, with its open views across a ha-ha, its distant prospect of mountains or sea, was what Swift particularly believed in. Visiting his friends at Market Hill in Co. Armagh, Sir Arthur and Lady Acheson, he satirizes his own obsession:

> How proudly he talks
> Of zigzacks and walks;
> And all the day raves
> Of cradles and caves;
> And boasts of his feats,
> His grottos and seats;
> Shews all his gew-gaws,
> And gapes for applause?
> A fine occupation
> For one of his station!
> A hole where a rabbit
> Would scorn to inhabit,
> Dug out in an hour
> He calls it a bow'r.
>
> from *My Lady's Lamentation and Complaint against the Dean*.

Beggar's Hut in Delville Gardens by Mrs Delany, 1745. The garden Swift most admired.

It was very much an age of poetry and gardens. Mrs Delany sketched the arbours and groves of Delville, young ladies were inspired by its temple. 'Hail happy *Delville*!' cried one, 'blissful Seat! The Muses's best belov'd retreat!' Nature was everywhere improved, the apprentice rhymester insisted, and 'raised by Art . . . blooming, and beautifully wild'.

But the Reverend Delany's living was now in the North of Ireland, and the enthusiasm of his horticultural partnership with Swift had all but beggared the poor man. Deploring his exile in Ulster, he miserably wrote:

> Add to this crying Grievance if you please,
> My horses founder'd on *Fermanagh* Ways;
> Ways of well-polish'd, and well-pointed Stone,
> Where every Step endangers every Bone;
> And more to raise your Pity, and your Wonder,
> Two Churches – twelve *Hibernian* Miles asunder!
> With complicated *Cures*, I labour hard in
> Besides whole Summers absent from my Garden!
>
> from *An Epistle.*

As he was wont to do, Swift laughed at his friend's predicament – but he never ceased to laugh at himself too. There is every sign that he considered himself something of a bore on the subject of gardens and at Market Hill he no doubt held forth greatly, advising and urging and condemning, as gardeners tend to. One imagines the long-suffering Achesons trailing behind him around their own garden while he redesigned it, filling it full of expensive shrubs and trees and brick-lined walls. The Achesons were the most patient of hosts and posterity is considerably in their debt, for Swift wrote some of his best verse at, or about, Market Hill. He also had a way of cutting down his hosts' trees when he considered it necessary.

> At *Market Hill*, as well appears
>   By Chronicle of antient Date,
> There stood for many a hundred Years
>   A spacious Thorn before the Gate.
>
> Hither came every Village Maid
>   And on the Boughs her Garland hung,
> And here beneath the spreading Shade,
>   Secure from Satyrs sat and sung.
>
> Sir *Archibald* that val'rous Knight,
>   The Lord of all the fruitful Plain,
> Would come to listen with Delight,
>   For he was fond of rural Strain.
>   · · ·
> But Time with Iron Teeth I ween
>   Has canker'd all its Branches round;
> No Fruit or Blossom to be seen,
>   Its Head reclining tow'rds the Ground.
>
> This aged, sickly, sapless Thorn
>   Which must alas no longer stand;
> Behold! the cruel Dean in Scorn
>   Cuts down with sacrilegious Hand.
>   from *On Cutting down the Old Thorn at Market Hill.*

The felling of the thorn tree displays Swift's purposeful, no-nonsense Protestantism in full confidence. Even though the spirit of Oisín had been effectively banished centuries ago, the old pagan superstitions which imbued natural phenomena with power still lingered. There would have been muttering indeed at Market Hill when the impatient Dean tidied away this

---

The Eagle's Nest, painting by Wm Sadler.

magic growth, for the thorn, above all trees, belonged to the otherworld. And what invective the neighbourhood's uneasiness must have inspired if word of it had reached the Achesons' drawing-room! The innocent hosts would have suffered first; no wonder Swift guessed that 'Lady A-S-N' grew weary of her obstreperous guest:

> Oh! if I could, how I would maul
>   His Tallow Face and Wainscot Paws,
> His Beetle-brows and Eyes of Wall,
>   And make him soon give up the Cause.
>
> from *Lady A-S-N Weary of the Dean.*

During the period of this famous friendship (Swift's visits to Co. Armagh took place between June 1728 and September 1730) he developed the eccentricities which in the end made ordinary social intercourse impossible for him. Being acutely aware of his own shortcomings simply wasn't enough, since he was incapable of doing anything about them.

> His manners would not let him wait,
>   Least we should think ourselves neglected,
> And so we saw him at our Gate
>   Three Days before he was expected.
>
> After a Week, a Month, a Quarter,
>   And Day succeeding after Day,
> Says not a word of his Departure
>   Tho' not a Soul would have him stay.

But if there were at that time few pens to match the barbed self-satire of Jonathan Swift's, the kind of gardens he delighted in were gradually establishing themselves all over Ireland. Kilruddery in Co. Wicklow, Headfort in Co Meath, Heywood, Adare, Ballyfin, Santry, Templeogue, Breckdenstown: the list goes on and on. Grottoes were studded with sea-shells, canals were dug, twenty-five whitened obelisks were raised on Lough Derg in Co. Clare, seats and statues and pillars discreetly sited. At Caledon in Co. Tyrone, Lord Orrery built a house of bones. 'We intend to strike the Caledonians with wonder and amazement, by affixing an ivory palace before their view. We have already gathered together great numbers of bones. Our friends the butchers and tanners of Tyrone have promised to increase the number.' Swift, making way for his elm trees in Dublin, might have supplied a few more.

But all this activity on the part of the Anglo-Irish well-to-do was accompanied by a certain lamentation. The poet Egan O'Rahilly (1670–1726)

Tipperary woodlands today.

had already claimed that 'foreign devils have made our land a tomb', and he cited in particular the new order imposed by a member of the Browne family in Co. Kerry. Under the Elizabethan settlement local people had been dispossessed ('Hamburg the refuge of him who has lost his land') as a result of lavish Crown grants. Gifts to the Brownes included the Lakes of Killarney, and similar generosity had improved the lot of the Herbert family. Nowhere in the world, perhaps, could have been more suitable for a burst of imperial splendour. Among the mountains and the lakes the Brownes' Kenmare House and the Herberts' Muckross magnificently rose, while Egan O'Rahilly deplored all that had been lost, rejecting the vulgarity of what seemed to him to be a *nouveau-riche* Munster.

> Fierce McCarthy Mór whose friends were welcome,
> McCarthy of the Lee a slave of late,
> McCarthy of Kanturk whose blood
> Has dried underfoot:
> Of all my princes not a single word –
> Irrevocable silence ails my heart.
>   . . .
>
> Take warning, wave, take warning, crown of the sea
> I, O'Rahilly – witless from your discords –
> Were Spanish sails again afloat
> And rescue on our tides,
> Would force this outcry down your wild throat,
> Would make you swallow these Atlantic words.
>   Translated from the Irish by Eavan Boland.

O'Rahilly spoke and wrote in Irish, and echoes of his protest fill the native literary vacuum during this long period of English aggrandizement. He owed allegiance to the Brownes, but he belonged in his heart to the dispossessed McCarthys. They were, as he would have put it, his true princes, and the culture they had left behind was only just managing to stagger on, like the Irish peasantry itself. Tenants were fortunate when a landowner bothered with his estate, because it meant that he bothered with them also. Thomas Browne, the fourth Earl of Kenmare, born the year Egan O'Rahilly died (1726), was such a figure, an 'easy, affable and polite man' who improved the fortunes of the little town of Killarney by introducing the manufacture of linen and woollen goods, supplying considerable employment by his extensive planting of his estates (a few of his oaks and limes are still there), and donating rustic seats and pavilions so that the townspeople might enjoy the view. He started a salmon fishery, and created a walk around Innisfallen, the largest island of the Lower Lake.

It was this particular island that Macaulay later declared to be 'not a reflex of heaven, but a bit of heaven itself', with its twelfth-century remains, its rowans

A view of the lower lake of Killarney by J. Fisher, 1796.

and its hollies. A contemporary visitor, Edward Willes, admired the hermitage Lord Kenmare was building there even though it was not large enough to 'admit room for more than one servant to wait inside so the side board was out of Doers and the wine served to us through the windows. . . . My Lord proposes building a room or two in the old Abbey style to retire to and spend a day when he pleases. I don't mean in the old Monkish Reverie and indolence, but with sensible cheerfulness accompanied with his friends.'

The whole island had been planted with potatoes 'to kill the Bryars and Thorns and [he] proposed having the whole next year in turf under the grove of Oak trees. There is likewise a large Rookery which adds greatly to the Beauty of the place. The whole Spot appears like Fairy Ground or the Inchanted Island. The ruins of the Abbey, The Hermitage cover'd with ivy as old as the Reformation. The Crawking of the Rooks, The different Romantic Scenes and views can't fail at putting me in mind of

In these deep Solitudes and Awful Cells
Where Heavenly pensive contemplation dwells etc.'

Muckross Abbey, watercolour by Wm Pars.

The other great family of Killarney, the Herberts, had incorporated a ruined Franciscan abbey as a folly on their estate at Muckross – and one begins to see Egan O'Rahilly's point of view. But relentlessly the Herberts advanced, and would have been amused no doubt to hear of the poet's spleen. Furze and brambles were cleared, huge rocks carted away, land drained, woods laid down, and the *Arbutus unedo*, the strawberry tree, lovingly cultivated.

The Killarney strawberry tree was later to catch the eye of Shelley when he stayed for a while on one of the islands and found the views more impressive than Switzerland's – perhaps because Switzerland didn't have those useful ruins which so prettily completed the picture and were an endless source of comment and conversation: Ross Castle of the O'Donoghues, Castle Lough of the McCarthys, the round tower at Aghadoe, the abbey of Innisfallen and the old friary that was the focal point at Muckross. When Arthur Young visited, there were even the bones of long-dead monks lying about, but these must have been later dealt with as efficiently as the boulders and brambles.

Carlyle, weary of hearing Killarney's praises, begged to be allowed to see the wonderland for himself: 'Don't bother me with audibly admiring it' – a sentiment which has had many an echo since. Bishop Berkeley was less impatient: 'The king of France,' he suggested, 'might lay out another Versailles, but . . . with all his revenues he could not lay out another Muckross.' Thackeray commented on the Torc Waterfall: 'Evergreens and other trees, in their brightest livery; blue sky; roaring water, here black and yonder foaming of a dazzling white; rocks shining in the dark places, or frowning black against the light, all the leaves and branches keeping up a perpetual waving and dancing round the cascade.'

It was probably a member of the Browne family who first made use of the echoes of the place in order to add a musical dimension to a Killarney sojourn. Trumpets were blown, later bugles. Tennyson was impressed:

> The splendour falls on castle walls
> And snowy summits old in story;
> The long light shakes across the lakes,
> And the wild cataract leaps in glory.
> Blow, bugle, blow, set the wild echoes flying,
> Blow bugle, answer, echoes, dying, dying, dying.

A view of Killarney's Turc Cascade (Torc Waterfall) by J. Fisher, 1790.

67

O hark, O hear! how thin and clear,
  And thinner, clearer, farther going!
O sweet and far from cliff and scar
  The horns of Elfland faintly blowing!
Blow, let us hear the purple glens replying;
Blow, bugle, answer, echoes, dying, dying, dying.

O love, they die in yon rich sky,
  They faint on hill or field or river:
Our echoes roll from soul to soul,
  And grow for ever and for ever.
Blow, bugle, blow, set the wild echoes flying,
And answer, echoes, answer, dying, dying, dying.

from *The Princess: A Medley.*

But the careful husbandry of Thomas Browne was not always, elsewhere, the order of the day. The new scourge of Ireland was the absentee landlord and in no time at all the Killarney trees were being cut down for timber. The woods had 'all gone to England', Lady Bessborough wrote to Lady Granville in 1808, giving the impression that a degree of indiscriminate chopping, lopping and thinning occurred whenever it was profitable. The felling of woodlands had also been long regretted by the native Irish. An anonymous seventeenth-century song – *The Tipperary Woodlands,* translated here by Frank O'Connor – had mourned less greedy times.

When once I rose at morning
The summer sun was shining,
I heard the horn awinding
  And birds' merry songs;
There were coney and beaver,
Woodcock and plover
And echo repeating
  The music of the guns;
The winded fox was flying,
Horsemen followed shouting,
Counting geese on the highway
  Some woman's heart was sore;
But now the woods are falling,
We must go over the water:
Shaun O'Dwyer of the Valley,
  Your pleasure is no more.

Cause enough for grieving,
My shelter a-felling,
The north wind freezing
  And death in the sky;

68

The garden of Thomas Browne's estate today.

My merry hound tied tightly
From sporting and chasing
That would lift a child's sorrow
    In noondays gone by.
The stag is on the mountain,
Swift and proud as ever;
He will come up the heather
    When our day is o'er.
All the woods are falling,
So we'll to the ships at Galway;
Shaun O'Dwyer of the Valley,
    Your pleasure is no more.

While the new English settlers were busy with their houses and gardens – or were guilty of neglecting them because it didn't cost so much – disaffection was periodically stifled, rebellion crushed. The ruthless Ulster plantation had been far more efficient than the plantations in Munster and Leinster, and had now been irreversibly established for many generations. The Penal Laws, which deprived Catholics of the rights of ordinary citizenship, were ruthless and efficient also, and for the poor there was little consolation to be found among the groves and temples that enhanced the landscape they shared with their masters: the vast majority of Irish peasants never laid eyes on them. 'Laws grind the poor,' as Goldsmith put it, 'and rich men rule the law': that was neatly true of the Ireland of this time, and was still to be so for many years to come.

Yet the native, underground voice continued; stories were told, poetry transcribed. The eighteenth-century Eileen O'Leary in *The Lament for Art O'Leary* tells of her husband's tribulations, which followed his reluctance to sell a horse to a Protestant for £5, a sum which the law obliged him to accept. Sorrowfully she mourns his murder at Carriganimma, Co. Cork, in 1773, recalling the places of their life together.

Could my calls but wake my kindred
In Derrynane beyond the mountains,
Or Capling of the yellow apples,
Many a proud and stately rider,
Many a girl with spotless kerchief,
Would be here before tomorrow,
Shedding tears about your body,
Art O'Leary, once so merry.

My love and my secret,
Your corn is stacked,
Your cows are milking;
On me is the grief
There's no cure for in Munster.
Till Art O'Leary rise
This grief will never yield
That's bruising all my heart
Yet shut up fast in it,
As 'twere in a locked trunk
With the key gone astray,
And rust grown on the wards.

My love and my calf,
Noble Art O'Leary,
Son of Conor, son of Cady,
Son of Lewis O'Leary,
West of the Valley
And east of Greenane
Where berries grow thickly
And nuts crowd on branches
And apples in heaps fall
In their own season;

Co. Mayo.

St Finbarr's Oratory, Gougane Barra, Co. Cork. Left: waterfall at Gougane Barra.

What wonder to any
If Iveleary lighted
And Ballingeary
And Gougane of the saints
For the smooth-palmed rider,
The unwearying huntsman
That I would see spurring
From Grenagh without halting
When quick hounds had faltered?
My rider of the bright eyes,
What happened you yesterday?
I thought you in my heart,
When I bought you your fine clothes,
A man the world could not slay.

from *The Lament for Art O'Leary*. Eileen O'Leary.
Translated from the Irish by Frank O'Connor.

Eileen O'Leary was the aunt of Daniel O'Connell, who was in time to bring about the emancipation of Irish – and English – Catholics. Her poem covers quite a large area of Co. Cork, visits the towns of Macroom and Millstreet, and moves west to Gougane Barra, the source of the River Lee. This strange, intense place is where St Finbarr, the patron saint of Cork, built a church on the rock of the lake. Either his presence or the great natural beauty of Gougane Barra lends it an atmosphere that is almost mystical. Pilgrimages are made to the islet and the ruins on Gougane Sunday, the first after the saint's feast day in September. Rather later than Eileen O'Leary (whose precise dates are not known), J. J. Callanan (1795–1829) wrote in English:

> There is a green island in lone Gougane Barra,
> Whence Allua of songs rushes forth like an arrow;
> In deep Valley Desmond a thousand wild fountains
> Come down to that lake, from their home in the mountains.
> There grows the wild ash; and a time-stricken willow
> Looks chidingly down on the mirth of the billow,
> As, like some gay child that sad monitor scorning,
> It lightly laughs back to the laugh of the morning.
>
> from *Gougane Barra*.

But the two poets who continued to keep the native culture alive more than anyone else were Anthony Raftery (1784–1835), the blind beggar-poet of the roads and the wilds, and Brian Merriman, who in 1781 finished his evocative *Midnight Court*. Raftery epitomizes the half-lost Ireland of his day, conjuring up places and landscapes which he never properly saw. He was himself of the Co. Mayo he honours here:

Now, with the coming in of the spring, the days will stretch a bit;
And after the Feast of Brigid I shall hoist my flag and go:
For, since the thought got into my head, I can neither stand nor sit
Until I find myself in the middle of the County of Mayo.

In Claremorris I should stop a night to sleep with decent men;
And then I'd go to Balla, just beyond, and drink galore;
And next I'd stay in Kiltimagh for about a month, and then
I should only be a couple of miles away from Ballymore!

I say and swear that my heart lifts up like the lifting of a tide;
Rising up like the rising wind till fog or mist must go,
When I remember Carra, and Gallen close beside,
And the Gap of the Two Bushes, and the wide plains of Mayo.

To Killaden then, to the place where everything grows that is best;
There are raspberries there, and strawberries there, and all that is good for men;
And were I only there, among my folk, my heart would rest,
For age itself would leave me there, and I'd be young again.

Translator unknown.

Brian Merriman (1747?–1805) was born in Co. Clare, the son of a small landowner. He became a teacher of mathematics and has left behind him the most extraordinary poem of the Irish eighteenth century. *The Midnight Court*, freely translated here by David Marcus, has been described by Professor Brendan Kennelly as pointing the way 'into a great deal of modern Irish writing, into the clumsy beginnings of a revival, into its gathering momentum and full flowering'. It catches, in its first lines, that mood of sleepy euphoria which sunshine and quiet countryside often induce.

> Beside the water I often walk
> Through fields where the dew is as thick as chalk;
> With the woods and the mountains just in sight
> I hang around for the dawn to light.
> Loch Greine lifts my soul with joy –
> Such land! Such country! What a sky!
> How silently the mountains rest
> Their heads upon each other's breast.
> This view would bring the heart to life –
> Be it worn with sickness, age, or strife –
> In the poorest beggar that ever stood
> Were he but to glance beyond the wood
> At the fleet of ducks, when the mist has gone,
> Convoyed by a single swan,
> And the jumping fish that shoot and flash
> High in the air with a rainbow splash,
> The blue of the lake and the breakers' roar
> Tossing and tumbling towards the shore;
> Birds on the branch that whistle and sing,
> Frolicking fawn that soar and spring,
> The sound of the horn and a glimpse of the hunt
> With the pack in chase and the fox in front.
>
> Yesterday, shooting from the east,
> And melting away the morning mist,
> The sunrays flashed and darted by,
> Burning a track across the sky.
> The nodding branches all around,
> The very grass upon the ground,
> The growth so green and flowers so fair
> Would soon dispel the worst despair.

But unease floats in from nowhere; a cloud shrouds the sun; thunder rattles on the lakeside shingle. Gone within a moment is the ferny idyll, the whistling birds, the frolicking fawn: all of a sudden, brutally even, *The Midnight Court* becomes one of the most perceptive accounts ever written of Irish sexual *mores*.

The poem tells of a visit in a dream to an eighteenth-century version of the old Celtic Sidhe, to an otherworld women's court that investigates the inbred desire of Irishmen to remain bachelors for as long as possible. A girl stands in the witness box, beautiful and tall, though clearly one who has suffered some disgrace, a wanton because no Irishman desires her. Why is it, she asks, that her

75

beauty awakes no passion? 'My mouth is sweet and my teeth are flashing.' Perplexed, she places beneath her pillow 'a stocking filled with freshest fruit'; on a road she spreads out flax, answering local superstition; in a heap of straw she sticks a cabbage head. But none of it works, no suitor proposes.

The girl is answered by an old man with a sharp line in invective, who postulates that all marriage is a snare and a trick. Since bastard children are as able and as attractive as those more legitimately born, why should a man tie himself up with a baggage who requires him to forget her past? Her easy ways, he insists, are known far and wide. She has been around:

> In Ibrickane with big and small,
> In Tirmaclane with one and all,
> In Kilbrickane with thick and thin,
> In Clare, in Ennis, and in Quin,
> In Cratlee and Tradree where they're tough
> She never seemed to have enough!

Though the racy style which charges the poem now is far removed from the lyricism with which Merriman cast his spell, there is a constant echo of nature itself, as a background to the natural forces that sport and play through the rhymes. The characters belong with the 'shapeless bracken' of the farmer's ancient song, with rocky earth, turf-bogs and barren hills. Such landscape is taken for granted, as all landscape is in the peasant world, but in the utterances of Merriman's people there is a perpetual closeness to the raw ground of the places that have shaped them. The poem idealizes, in its great fairy courtroom, the brutal facts of peasant life, but the facts remain. As Egan O'Rahilly did, it swipes at 'the upstart rogues' who have uprooted the old stock of Ireland; and it castigates, as well, the priests who have become their allies – a clerical ascendancy only a little more acceptable than the Protestant one.

Merriman's simplicity in a poem composed for peasants, and about peasants, is a continuation of the now long-established native Irish tradition: it would have been unusual had he written otherwise. The more sophisticated Congreve, on the other hand, who died twenty years before Merriman was born, is so entirely English in his writing that an Irish childhood – and education in Kilkenny and at Trinity College, Dublin – affected it hardly at all. George Farquhar, who was born in Derry in 1678 and also attended Trinity, belonged so much to the Establishment of the time that if Ireland is anywhere to be found in his work it is as a provincial outpost. Richard Brinsley Sheridan, who was born in Dublin in 1751, looked to England also. Unlike Swift, none of them regarded Ireland as a place to grow a garden in; none chose to live there and belong there.

But another Protestant, again of Trinity and of very roughly the same background and period, was not unaffected by his memories of Co. Westmeath in the 1740s. Goldsmith's *The Deserted Village*, once assumed to be simply a tale of a prosperous community's decline through some unexplained misfortune, tells of an Irish hamlet – though seeming now to be delicately English – that had been destroyed by the greed of an absentee landlord and the machinery of the Penal Laws. The Englishness of 'Sweet Auburn' is taken for granted because it is hard to imagine – and has been for more than two hundred years – in an Ireland that was destined to be so systematically exploited. Yet 'the tyrant's hand' and a beaten peasantry clearly belong in the Ireland of Goldsmith's time, and his own Lissoy in Co. Westmeath is so well charted in the Auburn of the poem that without great difficulty the site of mill and brook and church – even the Three Pigeons of *She Stoops to Conquer* – may still be found.

> Sweet Auburn! loveliest village of the plain,
> Where health and plenty cheered the labouring swain,
> Where smiling spring its earliest visit paid,
> And parting summer's lingering blooms delayed:
> Dear lovely bowers of innocence and ease,
> Seats of my youth, when every sport could please,
> How often have I loitered o'er thy green,
> Where humble happiness endeared each scene;
> How often have I paused on every charm,
> The sheltered cot, the cultivated farm,
> The never-failing brook, the busy mill,
> The decent church that topped the neighbouring hill,
> The hawthorn bush, with seats beneath the shade,
> For talking age and whispering lovers made!
> How often have I blessed the coming day,
> When toil remitting lent its turn to play,
> And all the village train, from labour free,
> Led up their sports beneath the spreading tree,
> While many a pastime circled in the shade,
> The young contending as the old surveyed,
> And many a gambol frolicked o'er the ground,
> And sleights of art and feats of strength went round,
> And still as each repeated pleasure tired,
> Succeeding sports the mirthful band inspired;
> The dancing pair that simply sought renown,
> By holding out, to tire each other down;
> The swain mistrustless of his smutted face,
> While secret laughter tittered round the place;
> The bashful virgin's sidelong looks of love,
> The matron's glance that would those looks reprove;
> These were thy charms, sweet village! sports like these
> With sweet succession, taught even toil to please;

These round thy bowers their cheerful influence shed,
These were thy charms – But all these charms are fled.
   Sweet smiling village, loveliest of the lawn,
Thy sports are fled, and all thy charms withdrawn;
Amidst thy bowers the tyrant's hand is seen,
And desolation saddens all thy green:
One only master grasps the whole domain,
And half a tillage stints thy smiling plain.
No more thy glassy brook reflects the day,
But, choked with sedges, works its weedy way
Along thy glades, a solitary guest,
The hollow-sounding bittern guards its nest;
Amidst thy desert walks the lapwing flies,
And tires their echoes with unvaried cries.
Sunk are thy bowers, in shapeless ruin all,
And the long grass o'ertops the mouldering wall,
And, trembling, shrinking from the spoiler's hand,
Far, far away, thy children leave the land.
   Ill fares the land, to hastening ills a prey,
Where wealth accumulates, and men decay;
Princes and lords may flourish, or may fade;
A breath can make them, as a breath has made:
But a bold peasantry, their country's pride,
When once destroyed, can never be supplied.

        from *The Deserted Village*. Oliver Goldsmith (1730–74).

Goldsmith bridges the gap between the native and the Anglo-Irish cultures. He laments in the Irish manner. He regrets the loss of an ideal past – one which may never have quite so purely existed – as the anonymous poets sometimes regretted the loss of a vigorous pre-Christian paganism. He keens over the dead, as the Tipperary woodlands were keened over. His nostalgia was anticipated by Egan O'Rahilly's bitter snarl that foreign devils had made his land a tomb, by the philosophical acceptance of Brian Merriman that Ireland's bones have been picked clean, and by the ubiquitous deploring of Norman Ireland cheapened.

The Goldsmiths were descended from a Catholic priest who turned to Protestantism in the middle of the seventeenth century, and they thereafter became a Church of Ireland family – which may be defined as a family in which poverty breeds a tendency to take holy orders. It certainly did so in the case of Oliver's father, a younger son without many prospects except those which had drifted on to the horizon with his marriage. A few fields could be managed without undue strain on his clerical duties, and when the Goldsmiths moved to Lissoy two years after Oliver's birth it was to a pleasant Queen Anne house, with a dairy and out-buildings, a garden and orchard. Even so, Irish clergymen rarely become rich, either through farming or by the Will of God, and the Reverend Goldsmith was no exception.

Lissoy became Oliver's universe. Already disintegrating as a village and a community, the most lively element left was possibly the chatty household of the rectory: sisters, brothers, servants in a modest way, a forceful mother, a good-natured father who none the less liked to insist that the wants of mankind should be our own. 'We were perfectly instructed in the art of *giving away* thousands,' the Man in Black of *The Citizen of the World* recalls, 'before we were taught the more necessary qualifications of *getting* a farthing.' But the little hamlet of Lissoy and the surrounding countryside, which is flat and undramatic, impinged as much as the Church of Ireland gossip of the rectory: all his life the easy landscape of his boyhood stirred Goldsmith's inspiration.

Part of that landscape was the great estate of Edgeworthstown, where Maria Edgeworth was destined to compose her 'moral tales' and to write *Castle Rackrent*, which, like *The Deserted Village*, tells of ruin and decay. Born in Oxfordshire in 1768, Maria Edgeworth came to Edgeworthstown when she was fifteen to help with the education of her brothers and sisters – which is how her moral tales began – and to assist her father in the running of his vast acreage. *Castle Rackrent* was a remarkably good read in its time, full of passion and attack, and to a considerable extent it remains so. But *Ormond*, a largely forgotten later novel, fastens more confidently on the roots of the Irish tragedy. Two cultures could not survive in so small an island, especially two cultures so separate and distinct. One had to go, and though Maria Edgeworth botched up a sloppy ending for this novel, her ear was close to the gound, even from within the confines of her father's parkland. Land, not landscaping, was what in the end was going to matter in Ireland: perfectly she understood that. In *Castle Rackrent* the young English wife, the heiress who is to save the house and the estate, is not enthusiastic about the prospects from the windows.

Then, by-and-by, she takes out her glass and begins spying over the country – 'And what's all that black swamp out yonder, Sir Kit?' says she – 'My bog, my dear,' says he, and went on whistling – 'It's a very ugly prospect, my dear,' says she – 'You don't see it, my dear, (says he) for we've planted it out, when the trees grow up, in summer time,' says he – 'Where are the trees, (said she) my dear?' still looking through her glass – 'You are blind, my dear, (says he) what are these under your eyes?' – 'These shrubs?' said she   'Trees,' said he – 'May be they are what you call trees in Ireland, my dear, (says she) but they are not a yard high, are they?' – 'They were planted out but last year, my lady' says I, to soften matters between them, for I saw she was going the way to make his honor mad with her – 'they are very well grown for their age, and you'll not see the bog of Allyballycarricko'shaughlin at all at all through the skreen, when once the leaves come out – But, my lady, you must not quarrel with any part or parcel of Allyballycarricko'shaughlin, for you don't know how many hundred years that same bit of bog has been in the family, we would not part with the bog of Allyballycarricko'shaughlin upon no account at all; it cost the late Sir Murtagh two hundred good pounds to defend his title to it, and boundaries, against the O'Learys, who cut a road through it.'

The truth was that the fine Georgian Ireland of the eighteenth century obscured a multitude of sins, and to that multitude was added in 1800 the Act of Union, in what now appears to have been a desperate attempt to prevent Ireland from slipping out of England's grasp. The terraces and crescents of Dublin and Limerick, the rose arbours, the small stately houses that were a pleasure to find at the end of country avenues, the orchards which had matured and borne plentiful fruit: all combined to form a handsome backdrop for the uneasy new century. But decay, long heralded and so increasingly an inspiration in Irish literature of both cultures, gathered a grotesque momentum, shadowing everywhere this era of vested interests and of landlords who added insult to injury by neglecting what their ancestors had been entrusted with. The failure of the rebellion of 1798, the stifling of Protestant leadership both in revolution and parliament, the plight of an Irish peasantry that was possibly the most wretched in Europe: all this in turn combined to spread the sour smell of hopelessness, and the feeling that the country was falling to pieces. In *Florence Macarthy*, a novel as forgotten as Maria Edgeworth's *Ormond*, its author, Lady Morgan, surveys the remnants of what the Fitzadlem family had once proudly delighted in:

Edgeworthstown, Co. Longford, home of Maria Edgeworth.
Opposite: Moydrum Castle, Co. Westmeath: monument to decay and neglect.

The massive stone pillars on either side, overgrown with lichens, still exhibited some vestiges of handsome sculpture; the capital of one was surmounted by a headless eagle, the other showed the claw and part of the body of a gos-hawk – both natives of the surrounding mountains, and well imitated in black marble, drawn from their once worked quarries. Two lodges mouldered on either side into absolute ruin, and the intended improvement of a Grecian portico to one, never finished, was still obvious in the scattered fragments of friezes and entablatures, which lay choked amidst heaps of nettles, furze-bushes, and long rye-grass. . . . The precipitous declivities which swept down from the rocky foundation of the house to the river, had been cut into terrace gardens, a fashion still observable at the seats of the ancient nobility of Munster: and it was melancholy to observe the stunted rose-tree, and other once-cultivated but now degenerate shrubs and flowers, raising their heads amongst nettles and briers, and long grass, and withered potatoe-stalks.

Historic Cashel, stronghold of Munster's kings, which had taken Christianity and the Normans in its easy stride, was entering another phase of its existence, that of the crumbling ancient monument. Sir Aubrey de Vere (1788–1846) mourned its nobility.

> Royal and saintly Cashel! I would gaze
>   Upon the wreck of thy departed powers,
>   Not in the dewy light of matin hours,
> Nor the meridian pomp of summer's blaze,
> But at the close of dim autumnal days,
>   When the sun's parting glance, through slanting showers,
>   Sheds o'er thy rock-throned battlements and towers
> Such awful gleams as brighten o'er Decay's
> Prophetic cheek. At such a time, methinks,
>   There breathes from thy lone courts and voiceless aisles
> A melancholy moral, such as sinks
>   On the lone traveller's heart, amid the piles
> Of vast Persepolis on her mountain stand,
> Or Thebes half buried in the desert sand.

The Rock of Cashel.

But all of it had been said before, by yet another of those anonymous poets who so loathed change and decay. Kilcash was a house of the Butlers, ancestral seat of an old Norman-Irish family, where the woods had been taken for timber. Little of the house's splendour remained; its bell had ceased to ring, and the lady who once had waited there, 'who shamed all women for grace', wasn't

---

The Rock of Cashel, Co. Tipperary.

even a ghostly presence any more. The nobility no longer visited. Mass was no longer said.

My grief and my affliction
    Your gates are taken away,
Your avenue needs attention,
    Goats in the garden stray.
The courtyard's filled with water
    And the great earls where are they?
The earls, the lady, the people
    Beaten into the clay.

No sound of duck or geese there,
    Hawk's cry or eagle's call,
No humming of the bees there
    That brought honey and wax for all,
Nor even the song of the birds there
    When the sun goes down in the west,
No cuckoo on top of the boughs there,
    Singing the world to rest.

There's mist there tumbling from branches,
    Unstirred by night and by day,
And darkness falling from heaven,
    For our fortune has ebbed away,
There's no holly nor hazel nor ash there,
    The pasture's rock and stone,
The crown of the forest has withered,
    And the last of its game is gone.

I beseech of Mary and Jesus
    That the great come home again
With long dances danced in the garden,
    Fiddle music and mirth among men,
That Kilcash the home of our fathers
    Be lifted on high again,
And from that to the deluge of waters
    In bounty and peace remain.

from *Kilcash*. Anonymous, 18th century.
Translated from the Irish by Frank O'Connor

Kilcash Castle, Co. Tipperary, built *c.* 1544, ancestral seat of the Butler family.

The Uneasy 19th Century

Mr and Mrs S. C. Hall were the most devoted of the Victorians who wrote about 'Ireland: its scenery, character, etc.' They took the map county by county, left scarcely a stone in the entire country unturned, listened to the anecdotage they were plied with, supplied a historical background when they thought it to be judicious, and commented upon the untutored condition of the locals. They were a fastidious, painstaking, and by all accounts curious pair.

Anna Maria Fielding, as she'd been, spent her childhood in Co. Wexford, later marrying the pious Samuel Carter Hall – said to have been the model for Pecksniff in *Martin Chuzzlewit*. In doing so she chose a partner who shared her evangelical spirit and brisk commercial sense, and together they became as professional a couple of travel writers as you'd find anywhere today. Although they presented nothing that was 'prejudicial to the United Kingdom', their *Ireland: Its Scenery, Character, etc.* has remained justly prominent as a reflection of the developing tourist attitude to a country that was, above all else, 'picturesque'. The English aristocracy had made it so, landscaping and exploiting a natural grandeur. 'We repeat,' insisted the Halls, 'there is no country in the world so safe or so pleasant for strangers; while so abundant is the recompense of enjoyment it can supply, that for every new visitor it receives, it will obtain a new friend.'

When the Halls journeyed through a county they didn't think much of, they abruptly dismissed it and filled the chapter planned for its description with something else: 'As the county presents no particular feature for comment, we shall avail ourselves of the opportunity for offering some observations relative to the dwellings of the humbler, or working, classes, in Ireland.'

While accounting Sligo 'rich in the picturesque', it is – say the Halls – so like its neighbouring Mayo that 'we pass over Sligo'. There then follows a long and not at all uninteresting story about one of its 'wild and lawless' sons, a poteen manufacturer known as Hill Murphy. Such tales – of family violence, jealousy or pride, half factual half apocryphal – were another element in the picturesque for the visitor to cherish, and an element also in the literature of the time. The blarney and the begorrah, which have so bedevilled Irish writing ever since, were born of whimsy and a desire to please the visitor or the family of the big house. Among country people in Ireland there is still today a desire to tell the stranger what he most wishes to hear, and there is everywhere the residue of an innate inferiority complex in both life and art.

But it was hardly recognized as that by such distinguished British writers as Sir Walter Scott, Wordsworth, Tennyson, Shelley, Thackeray and Trollope, all of whom were duly impressed by most of what they encountered. For Scott, the scenery of Kerry was the 'grandest sight I have ever seen'. Trollope, especially in his novel *The Kellys and the O'Kellys*, displayed a swiftly acquired grasp of the nuances and subtleties of the Irish life he came to know while a Post Office official in Banagher and later Clonmel. Ireland had rescued him from a life of office drudgery in London, and he never ceased to be grateful. 'Who has had,' he afterwards wondered, 'a happier life than mine?' Hunting, wining and dining, fascinated by Irish country ways, Trollope soon became typical of another generation that found England's second island very much the invigorating resort the Halls described. And Thackeray, in his *Irish Sketch-Book*, was just as struck. Of Glendalough in Co. Wicklow he noted that 'Directly you see it, it smiles at you as innocent and friendly as a little child; and once seen it becomes your friend for ever, and you are always happy when you think of it.'

Glendalough was very much on the tourist route, together with the Rock of Cashel and Killarney, the Ring of Kerry, the Cliffs of Moher, Connemara and Mayo, Donegal, the Giant's Causeway, the Antrim coast road. When visiting the renowned Causeway, the Halls advise the tourist to make the whiskey town of Bushmills 'his abiding place' and recommend a hotel for its 'neatness, cleanliness, and good order, the attention, zeal, and kindliness of its landlady, and the exceeding moderation of her charges'. The Causeway itself they consider 'one of the wonders of the world', and in its way it probably is, a basaltic marvel which put Thackeray in touch with the beginning of creation.

A pleasure boat
at the
Giant's Causeway.

87

The sea looks older than in other places, the hills and rocks strange, and formed differently from other rocks and hills. . . . The hill-tops are shattered into a thousand cragged fantastical shapes. . . . The savage rock-sides are painted of a hundred colours. Does the sun ever shine here? When the world was moulded and fashioned out of formless chaos, this must have been the *bit over* – a remnant of chaos!

from *Irish Sketch-Book*.

Hotels sprang up everywhere to cater for the delighted travellers, and there was an abundance of eager guides to instruct them. 'The Kerry and Wicklow guides,' noted Mr and Mrs Hall, 'delight in legends of fays and fairies, in snatches of songs, bits of ballads, and in impossibilities of all kinds; there is nothing too wild and wonderful for them – nothing too airy or fantastic; their wit and their rags flutter together; they greet you with a jest, and bid you farewell with a tear. Not so the northern guides: they are, from Neil MacMullen – the protector of the Causeway, being so appointed by the noble family of Antrim – down to the smallest cragsman – to the tiny boy who hops like a young sea-bird from rock to rock, people of knowledge – geologists, learned in the names of stones, and conversant with stratas and basalts; stiff and steady; observant and particular – they love to be particular – they are remarkable for the exactness and minutiae of their details; they talk with a profound air of hexagons and octagons, and when they excite an exlamation of wonder, they never sympathise with it, but treat it as a matter of course that you should be the astonished, and they the astonishers.'

Gerald Griffin, author of *The Collegians* and, more impressively, of the collection of stories called *Holland-Tide*, was born in Limerick in 1803. He knew, intimately, the provincial and rural people he wrote about, and in his perception of the landscape of Munster there is often an ominous note. 'In a lonely cabin, in a lonely glen, on the shores of a lonely lough, in one of the most lonesome districts of west Munster, lived a lone woman named Guare . . .'

In *The Aylmers of Bally-Aylmer* Mrs Giltinaan, 'hostess of an humble inn on the west border of Limerick', encounters a young gentleman 'whose sharp accent and smart dress bespoke a recent acquaintance with Dublin life'. In other words he doesn't know his way about the countryside, is not protected by guides or companions or even by daylight. Mrs Giltinaan is horrified.

'The mountains! The Kerry hills! Alone by yourself, and at this time o'night! – Now, hear to me, will you, sir, for it's a lonesome way you're taking, and them mountains is the place for all manner of evil doings from the living and the dead.

The Giant's Causeway, Co. Antrim.

Take this little bottle of holy water, and shake a little upon your forehead, when you step upon the heath. Walk on bold and straight before you, and if the dead night come upon you, which I hope no such thing will happen till you reach Tralee any way, you won't whistle, don't, for it is that calls 'em all about one if they do be there; you know who I mean, sir. If you chance to see or hear any thing bad, you have only to hold these beads up over your head and stoop under it, and whatever it is, must pass over the beads without doing you any harm . . .'

The solitary traveller, and the adventures that might befall him, is a favourite figure in Irish literature; so, too, is the creature who suddenly appears, as if emerging from some part of the landscape itself – hermit, ghost, hedge-schoolmaster on the run, rebel left over from 1798. The eeriness that is still to be found on the mist-clad summit of Lugnaquilla, or the high slopes of the MacGillycuddy Reeks, or in the glens of almost every Irish county, was well understood by John Banim, a contemporary of Griffin's:

Up the valley, far as my eye could travel, and at last, over the broad bosom of the distant hill, which seemed torn and indented with the headlong torrent it had once poured down, far and uniform on every side a verticular July sun was shining. The whole effect was fiercely brilliant, and so unbroken, that a sparrow could not have hopped, or a grass-mouse raced across, even in the distance, without being immediately detected as an intrusion upon the scene; as a sudden speck with which nothing else must have held any relation or keeping.

The desertion and silence of the place, sympathized well with its lethargic features; the peasant seemed to have shunned it . . . as haunted or unholy ground. Not a single cabin met my eye through the range of the valley; over head, indeed, the gables of one or two peeped down, half hidden by their sameness of colour with the weather-tanned rocks on which they hung, or with the heather that thatched them; but they and their inmates were obviously unconnected with the solitude in which I stood . . . No moving thing animated my now almost supernatural picture; no cow, horse, nor sheep, saunteringly grazed along the margin of my wizard stream. The very little birds flew over it, I conveniently thought, with an agitated rapidity, or if one of them alighted on the shrivelled spray, it was but to look around for a moment with a keen mistrustful eye; and then bound into his fields for air, leaving the wild branch slightly fluttered by his action. If a sound arose, it was but what its own whispering waters made; or the herdsboy's whistle faintly echoed from far-off fields and meadows; or the hoarse and lonesome caw of the rook, as he winged his heavy flight towards some fertile place.

Amid all this light and silence, a very aged woman, wildly habited, appeared, I know not how, before me . . .

from *The Fetches*.

Above: the lonely Kerry hills.
Below: Glendalough, Co. Wicklow.

Brian Merriman begins *The Midnight Court* with a similar visitation, a creature 'in the shape of a woman approaching me'. And James Clarence Mangan translates the eighteenth-century Brian O'Flaherty:

> The birds carolled songs of delight
> And the flowers bloomed bright on my path
> As I stood all alone on the height
> Where rises Bruff's old faery rath.
>
> Before me unstirred by the wind
> The beautiful lake lay outspread
> Whose waters give sight to the blind
> And would almost awaken the dead.
>
> As I gazed on the silvery stream
> So loved by the heroes of old
> There neared me as though in a dream
> A maiden with tresses of gold.

'It is indeed rare,' wrote the Halls, 'to pass a single mile without encountering an object to which some marvellous fiction is attached. Every lake, mountain, ruin of church or castle, rath and boreen, has its legendary tale; the Fairies people every wild spot; the Banshee is the follower of every old family; Phookas and Cluricannes are – if not to be seen, to be heard of, in every solitary glen.'

The vulgarized 'fairies', the 'little people' and leprechauns, in fact disguise an inbred fear of dislocated spirits. Nourished by the veneration of the Celts, surviving the coming of Christianity, to this day a thread winds back to the graves of Ireland's earliest inhabitants. Irish fairy rings – more evidence of the picturesque for the Victorian visitor – do not suggest the prettily winged fairies of Peter Pan or the elves of Alfred Lord Tennyson or William Allingham's 'little men' of the airy mountain: they imply the unknown, and the proximity of an undefined evil.

Trees play a particular part in all this. They carry spells, are enchanted, holy, unlucky, to be avoided or cautiously approached. Their berries promise fertility; there are portents in the patterns of their branches, symbols in their leaves and trunks. Over and over again, insistently, repetitiously, trees push themselves to the Irish forefront. Trees planted, trees cut down; Spenser's trees, Sweeney's trees, Swift's trees; Seamus Heaney's 'god in the tree, impalpable perhaps but still indigenous, less doctrinally defined than the god of the monasteries but more intuitively apprehended. The powers of the Celtic otherworld hovered there.'

Sacred hawthorn trees, Co. Westmeath.

'Get up, our Anna dear, from the weary spinning-wheel;
　　For your father's on the hill, and your mother is asleep:
Come up above the crags, and we'll dance a highland reel
　　Around the fairy thorn on the steep.'

At Anna Grace's door 'twas thus the maidens cried,
　　Three merry maidens fair in kirtles of the green;
And Anna laid the rock and the weary wheel aside,
　　The fairest of the four, I ween.

They're glancing through the glimmer of the quiet eve,
　　Away in milky wavings of neck and ankle bare;
The heavy-sliding stream in its sleepy song they leave,
　　And the crags in the ghostly air:

And linking hand and hand, and singing as they go,
　　The maids along the hill-side have ta'en their fearless way,
Till they come to where the rowan trees in lonely beauty grow
　　Beside the Fairy Hawthorn grey.

The Hawthorn stands between the ashes tall and slim,
　　Like matron with her twin grand-daughters at her knee;
The rowan berries cluster o'er her low head grey and dim
　　In ruddy kisses sweet to see.

The merry maidens four have ranged them in a row,
    Between each lovely couple a stately rowan stem,
And away in mazes wavy, like skimming birds they go,
    Oh, never caroll'd bird like them!

But solemn is the silence of the silvery haze
    That drinks away their voices in echoless repose,
And dreamily the evening has still'd the haunted braes,
    And dreamier the gloaming grows.

And sinking one by one, like lark-notes from the sky
    When the falcon's shadow saileth across the open shaw,
Are hush'd the maidens' voices, as cowering down they lie
    In the flutter of their sudden awe.

For, from the air above, and the grassy ground beneath,
    And from the mountain-ashes and the old whitethorn between,
A Power of faint enchantment doth through their beings breathe,
    And they sink down together on the green.

They sink together silent, and stealing side to side,
    They fling their lovely arms o'er their drooping necks so fair,
Then vainly strive again their naked arms to hide,
    For their shrinking necks again are bare.

Thus clasp'd and prostrate all, with their heads together bow'd,
    Soft o'er their bosoms' beating – the only human sound –
They hear the silky footsteps of the silent fairy crowd,
    Like a river in the air, gliding round.

No scream can any raise, nor prayer can any say,
    But wild, wild, the terror of the speechless three –
For they feel fair Anna Grace drawn silently away,
    By whom they dare not look to see.

They feel their tresses twine with her parting locks of gold,
    And the curls elastic falling, as her head withdraws;
They feel her sliding arms from their tranced arms unfold,
    But they may not look to see the cause:

For heavy on their senses the faint enchantment lies
    Through all that night of anguish and perilous amaze;
And neither fear nor wonder can ope their quivering eyes
    Or their limbs from the cold ground raise,

Till out of night the earth has roll'd her dewy side,
    With every haunted mountain and streamy vale below;
When, as the mist dissolves in the yellow morning tide,
    The maidens' trance dissolveth so.

Then fly the ghastly three as swiftly as they may,
    And tell their tale of sorrow to anxious friends in vain —
They pined away and died within the year and day,
    And ne'er was Anna Grace seen again.
        The Fairy Thorn. Samuel Ferguson (1810–86), from an Ulster ballad.

Samuel Ferguson was born in Belfast and died in Dublin. He was a lawyer and archaeologist, and Deputy Keeper of the Records of Ireland. In spite, however, of seeming to be part of the nineteenth-century Establishment, he supported the Irish cause, and in particular the Young Irelanders, among whom Thomas Davis was a leading light. These young men, mainly Protestant and successors to Wolfe Tone's United Irishmen, found their inspiration in the past, in the old Gaelic and Norman Ireland. Songs, ballads and poems urged them on their revolutionary way, but the early death of Thomas Davis and, in the same September (1845), the first ominous signs of the potato failure that led to the Great Famine robbed the movement of its vigour. Samuel Ferguson wrote of the corn that was later, at the height of that disaster, still being exported; but he was really lamenting the death of one of Ireland's most attractive political leaders.

I walked through Ballinderry in the springtime,
    When the bud was on the tree,
And I said, in every fresh-ploughed field beholding
    The sowers striding free,
Scattering broadcast forth the corn in golden plenty,
    On the quick, seed-clasping soil,
'Even such this day among the fresh-stirred hearts of Erin,
    Thomas Davis, is thy toil!'
                            from *Lament for the Death of Thomas Davis.*

Lady Wilde, Oscar Wilde's mother and the 'Speranza' who wrote razorlike political comment for the Young Irelanders' paper, the *Nation,* painted a grimmer picture:

Weary men, what reap ye? — 'Golden corn for the stranger.'
What sow ye? — 'Human corses that await for the Avenger.'
Fainting forms, all hunger-stricken, what see you in the offing?
'Stately ships to bear our food away amid the stranger's scoffing.'
There's a proud array of soldiers — what do they round your door?
'They guard our master's granaries from the thin hands of the poor.'
                            from *The Famine Year.*

Spared the industrial revolution, Ireland escaped its Satanic mills, its furnaces that must not ever die out as in Dickens's *Old Curiosity Shop,* its bleak expansion of provincial towns. But at the end of the eighteenth century the landscape had changed in another way, for before that time Samuel Ferguson would not have written as naturally of 'corn in golden plenty' nor Lady Wilde of her 'golden corn for the stranger'. It was Foster's Corn Law of 1784, passed to protect the home market by excluding all foreign grain, that had swiftly turned Ireland into a land of tillage and wheat fields.

Yet when the famine came the existing trade pattern by which Irish grain was automatically sent to England was not broken; nor could Indian corn be imported to feed a dying nation until, too late, the Corn Laws were repealed. The cold, hungry winters of 1846 and 1847 dramatically changed the face of Ireland all over again. Death and emigration reduced the population from eight million to five, and the boom years of the protected corn harvests were over. The wandering harvesters, profitably on the move from farm to farm with their scythes, the burgeoning acres of tillage, the relative prosperity of smallholders, and the hopeful chance that if the riches could be shared with the better landlords there might even be an end to disaffection: all that disappeared as the Great Famine ruthlessly clawed open the Irish wound.

William Carleton (1794–1869) wrote bitterly of the Famine's excesses. In many ways the most interesting of the nineteenth-century novelists and short-story writers who did not belong to the Ascendancy class, Carleton was, like Samuel Ferguson, essentially of Ulster. In *Poor Scholar*, the novelist Benedict Kiely writes of Carleton's South Tyrone:

> It is not mountainy land. It is not flat land. The tarred roads, linking the little towns together, rise and fall regularly over round rich hills, farmed to the top, held in place by a network of deep whispering hedges. Here and there the primitive force of the earth revolts from rich greenery, from fruitful furrows drawn by the rigid coulter; rises up into sombre moorland, or a ridge covered with coarse heather, or a hill planted with straight trees. The roads rise and fall, dropping into little glens where the leaves and the roadside grasses are unbelievably quiet, going over round hills to open up visions of infinite blue distances, with mountains very low and far away on an uncertain horizon. Under a sultry sky on a warm July day the place has something symbolic of everything in the genius of the man that the place made: richness and colour in the good, farmed land; in the moors and the occasional rocks something unkempt and desolate and always out of control; in those blue, infinite spaces some suggestion of greatness and power, never exactly defined, never stabilised and made permanent.

The son of a small tenant farmer, Carleton wished to become a priest but his father was unable to afford the expenses involved, and at the same time the family was evicted. His peasant background, the rough culture of his Irish-speaking parents, his education in hedge-schools, and the down-to-earth landscape of Tyrone, all stood him in good stead when he came to write his first short stories. He took to the roads when the family found itself destitute, a

Young husbandman of Erin's fruitful seed-time,
In the fresh track of danger's plough!
Who will walk the heavy, toilsome perilous furrow
Girt with freedom's seed-sheets now?

(*Lament for the Death of Thomas Davis*: Samuel Ferguson)

roaring giant of a man who drank and whored his way from Ulster to Dublin, encountering on his journey many of the characters who were later to feature in his fiction. These perpetual travellers were rather different from their English equivalents, as described by Dickens. There's an exotic sophistication about Short and Codlin, for instance, about Jerry and his Dancing Dogs, Mrs Jarley and Mr Vuffin, a quality that would hardly have been found in the victims of eviction and famine or in the out-of-work 'spalpeens' – the scythe-men who had earned well in the time of the Corn Laws – or in the spirits whom Gerald Griffin's Mrs Giltinaan had warned against. There was violence everywhere, but in their promotion of Ireland the Halls were not being disingenuous when they declared the country so very safe: for the tourists they addressed it probably was. But not for the homeless in search of shelter, nor for Carleton himself. In one of his finest stories, a chilly tale of multiple murder, he doesn't spare the sensibilities, firmly relating his fiction to the facts it springs from:

> This tale of terror is, unfortunately, too true. The scene of hellish murder detailed in it lies at Wildgoose Lodge in the county of Louth, within about four miles of Carrickmacross, and nine of Dundalk. No such multitudinous murder has occurred, under similar circumstances, except the burning of the Sheas in the county of Tipperary. The name of the family burned in Wildgoose Lodge was Lynch. One of them had, shortly before this fatal night, prosecuted and convicted some of the neighbouring Ribbonmen, who visited him with severe marks of their displeasure in consequence of his having refused to enrol himself as a member of their body.

from *Wildgoose Lodge.*

Like Griffin and Banim, Carleton through necessity became a hack. He also, having fallen in love with a Protestant girl, became a Protestant. His life was not easy, and there cannot have been an instant response to much of what he wrote. Circumstances fashioned his talent, he picked up a living as best he could, and in spite of adversity left behind a rare and intimate picture of a peasantry's desperation. He died a melancholy drunkard in Dublin in 1869, perhaps recalling through the last of his whiskey mists the modest beauty of his Clogher valley.

By now, among Irish writers, there was increasingly a fusing of national feeling with the landscape that made Ireland Ireland. Patriotism and mountains, freedom and the familiar fields, history and geography: these were two sides of a coin that had been there for many centuries but had recently been given a fresh gleam. James Clarence Mangan, seeming to personify Ireland in *Dark Rosaleen,* did not make a woman of her but rather a place possessed by a woman's spirit. And in his *Lament for the Princes of Tir-Owen and Tirconnell* all Ireland is affectionately embraced in the woe of mourning:

Lough Erne at Ely Lodge, Co. Fermanagh.

Beside the wave, in Donegal,
    In Antrim's glen, or fair Dromore,
        Or Killillee,
Or where the sunny waters fall
    At Assaroe, near Erna's shore,
        This could not be.
On Derry's plains – in rich Drumcliff –
    Throughout Armagh the Great, renowned
        In olden years,
No day could pass but woman's grief
    Would rain upon the burial-ground
        Fresh floods of tears!

Oh no! – from Shannon, Boyne, and Suir,
    From high Dunluce's castle-walls,
        From Lissadill,
Would flock alike both rich and poor.
    One wail would rise from Cruachan's halls
        To Tara's hill;
And some would come from Barrow-side,
    And many a maid would leave her home
        On Leitrim's plains,
And by melodious Banna's tide,
    And by the Mourne and Erne, to come
        And swell thy strains!

And Samuel Ferguson:

I stood on Derrybawn in the autumn,
    I heard the eagle call,
With a clangorous cry of wrath and lamentation
    That filled the wide mountain hall,
O'er the bare, deserted place of his plundered eyric,
    And I said, as he screamed and soared,
'So callest thou, thou wrathful-soaring Thomas Davis,
    For a nation's rights restored.'

                    from *Lament for the Death of Thomas Davis.*

Emigration and homesickness fuelled such images. In America, and to a lesser extent all over the world, Ireland was remembered with fondness – and with an anger not yet entirely extinguished. 'In woeful plight' the exile of George Fox's poem sailed glumly away from 'Sweet Mayo', already donating his bones to a grave in Santa Cruz. Francis Sylvester Mahony, famous in his time as 'Father Prout', remained faithful in doggerel to the church bells of Cork.

There is another corner of Cork I love, and late at night, preferably a Sunday night, when everything is heavy with silence, I will be under Shandon in the narrow street . . . and the only sound is the deep boom of the bell's toll overhead. (An Irish Journey: Sean O'Faolain)

View of the city of Cork by Thomas Sautell Roberts, 1799.

There's a bell in Moscow, while on tower and Kiosko
  In St Sophia the Turkman gets,
And loud in air calls men to prayer
  From the tapering summit of tall minarets.
Such empty phantom I freely grant' em,
    But there's an anthem more dear to me:
      'Tis the bells of Shandon,
        That sound so grand on
  The pleasant waters of the river Lee.

In *The Winding Banks of Erne* William Allingham (1824–89) forgets nothing: the summer crowds at Bundoran, shells gathered on the beach, the boats, the crabs, the sloping fields, the lofty rocks 'where ash and holly grow', and the yew tree 'gazing on the curving flood below'. With sorrowful reluctance he bids farewell to Ballyshannon in seaside Donegal and the magnificence of Lough Erne.

Adieu to Belashanny! where I was bred and born;
Go where I may, I'll think of you, as sure as night and morn,
The kindly spot, the friendly town, where every one is known,
And not a face in all the place but partly seems my own;
There's not a house or window, there's not a field or hill,
But, east or west, in foreign lands, I'll recollect them still.
I leave my warm heart with you, tho' my back I'm forced to turn –
Adieu to Belashanny, and the winding banks of Erne!

More grimly, in *Tenants at Will*, from *Lawrence Bloomfield in Ireland*, Allingham tells of an eviction:

> In early morning twilight, raw and chill,
> Damp vapours brooding on the barren hill,
> Through miles of mire in steady grave array
> Threescore well-arm'd police pursue their way;
> Each tall and bearded man a rifle swings,
> And under each greatcoat a bayonet clings . . .

All that, too, was remembered and related wherever the exile found himself, in Chicago or New South Wales, in Montreal or Karikal. The sweeping beauty of Clare or Galway, afternoons in Lismore, haymaking by the Shannon, the turf gathered in from the Wicklow bogs, the salmon leaping in the Slaney: nostalgia was painful, no doubt, but not as painful as the scenes from which good fortune had permitted an escape. Allingham's poem continues:

> The Hamlet clustering on its hill is seen,
> A score of petty homesteads, dark and mean;
> Poor always, not despairing until now;
> Long used, as well as poverty knows how,
> With life's oppressive trifles to contend.
> This day will bring its history to an end.

> *Mere shattered walls, and doors with useless latch*
> *And firesides buried under fallen thatch.*
> (*Tenants at Will*: William Allingham)

In England in 1811 *Sense and Sensibility* was published; in 1839 *Nicholas Nickleby*; in 1848 *Vanity Fair*; in 1871 *Middlemarch*. The genius of the Brontës flowered; there were Lewis Carroll and Mrs Gaskell and Robert Louis Stevenson.

Nothing to match that literary explosion came out of Ireland, and the reason is a fairly straightforward one. Victorian England was like a great mahogany edifice, enriched with curlicues and secret places, with frills and antimacassars to hide what was best not seen. All the time in the world was at the disposal of the people at the hub of Victoria's empire, bolstered by as much confidence as the ruling classes could comfortably sustain. It was the perfect hierarchical environment for long afternoons of cricket, for keeping up the eighteenth-century gardens that were decaying in Ireland, for writing and reading the novels that were edifices in themselves. Ireland, compared, lay in fragments, a battleground for seven centuries, a provincial wilderness beyond the pale of Dublin and the life of the big country houses, sick at heart and with half of its population starving. It had neither the mood nor the stomach for a new art form, just as it hadn't the leisure for the ceremony and subtlety of the game of cricket. Like the novel, that sport has since only intermittently flourished in Ireland.

But there was, of course, some nineteenth-century literary activity of a more innovatory kind than fireside storytelling or the exile's elegy. As well as the sophistications of Maria Edgeworth, there was the contribution of the rumbustious medic, Charles Lever (1806–72), and that of the more serious Charles Kickham (1828–82). They wrote novels that were as different as they themselves were, but neither acquired the sure touch of Sheridan Le Fanu (1814–73), whose *Uncle Silas*, though set in England, is haunted by its author's Irishness. At the tail-end of the century Somerville and Ross (Edith Oenone Somerville, 1858–1949; Violet Martin, 1862–1915) published *The Real Charlotte*, an Ascendancy novel of very considerable quality. But that renowned partnership belongs more correctly to the future.

During all this time the oral tradition of the old storytellers, the *seanchaidhe*, persisted, as did the forbidden Irish language. The result was that, with a debilitating effect, two cultures pulled in two different directions, as Maria Edgeworth had sensed they would. Irish literature in the early and middle nineteenth century is illuminated mainly by miniatures, by moments and flashes, bits and pieces. It would have sounded like a joke to have said they heralded a renaissance.

Within the still vigorous Anglo-Irish tradition Somerville and Ross began to write about their Irish RM, a resident magistrate who has been a model ever since for the well-intentioned gullible Englishman on the loose in Ireland (*Some Experiences of an Irish R.M.*, 1899; *Further Experiences of an Irish R.M.*, 1908).

Drishane, Co. Cork, seat of the Somerville family.

Lesser writers such as Dorothea Conyers, forgotten now, and George Birmingham occupy the same realm, the literary accent on fun and funniness, on the likable devil-may-care Irish of the lower orders, the impoverished Anglo-Irish and the bewildered English.

The Somervilles were of Castletownshend, a harbour village near Skibbereen in Co. Cork. 'An unusual sort of place,' Maurice Collis writes in his biography of the two women, 'because half a dozen families of the Cork landed gentry were settled there, instead of living as the Irish landed gentry generally did, on estates dotted about the counties, miles apart from each other . . .

The site was high ground which shelved steeply to the sea, a deep inlet or haven from the Atlantic like many others in western Cork. The view from the houses down to the haven and out to its mouth on the ocean was very fine. Near the west entrance to the village, a high point on the site, stood Drishane, the seat of the Somerville family. The avenue gate to Glen Barrahane, the seat of the Coghills, was just below. Standing on the shore of the haven to the eastward was the Castle, the seat of the Townshends. These were the leading families, heads of which had held at times the office of High Sheriff of the County of Cork and also high rank in the British army and navy. During the eighteenth and nineteenth centuries they intermarried.

But the Martin family, though related, were not of Castletownshend. Violet Martin was born at Ross House, near Oughterard in Co. Galway, the youngest child of James Martin. 'During the eighteenth century,' Maurice Collis continues, 'the Martins had been the greatest landed magnates in Connaught. They were of Norman origin. Oliver Martin, who was to found the Irish family, went as a youthful Norman squire to the Holy Land with Richard Coeur de Lion, who granted him a coat of arms with the motto: "Sic itur ad astra."'

Hunting is at the heart of the RM stories – landscape on the hoof, hedges and ditches seen from hunting's angle:

> I cantered over the ridge of the hill, and down it towards the cottage near which I was accustomed to get out on to the road again. As I neared my wonted opening in the fence, I saw that it had been filled by a stout pole, well fixed into the bank at each end, but not more than three feet high. Cruiskeen pricked her ears at it with intelligence; I trotted her at it, and gave her a whack.
>
> Ages afterwards there was someone speaking on the blurred edge of a dream . . .
>
> from *A Misdeal.*

Even a drive in a dogcart acquires a sporting flavour:

> It was a long drive, twelve miles at least, and a very cold one. We passed through long tracts of pasture country, fraught, for Flurry, with memories of runs, which were recorded for me, fence by fence, in every one of which the biggest dog-fox in the country had gone to ground, with not two feet – measured accurately on the handle of the whip – between him and the leading hound; through bogs that imperceptibly melted into lakes, and finally down and down into a valley, where

Experiences of leisured Irish writers: Miss Somerville, centre, and Miss Violet Martin (Ross) second from right, in white.

Landscape near Castletownshend, Co. Cork.

the fir-trees of Aussolas clustered darkly round a glittering lake, and all but hid the grey roofs and pointed gables of Aussolas Castle.

from *Trinket's Colt.*

The Great War drew vast numbers of the same devil-may-care Irish into the ranks of British regiments. It also supplied the opportunity for Ireland's long-promised revolution. This one turned out to be, to some extent, successful; the infamous Black and Tans who were hurried across the Irish Sea to settle the Irish hash in a swift Cromwellian manner failed to do so; the nationalism which flickered on the streets of Dublin in 1916 later burnt its way through the country, which later still survived a civil war and finally found itself — all but for six Northern counties — unshackled from the British Empire. But it was far from a satisfactory outcome. The partition of Ireland, arbitrarily fixed, was a hasty and desperate arrangement that stands today as a reminder of an ancient plantation, for ever driving a wedge between the people of an unsettled province.

The Infant Nation

YET EVEN AS that inept political division was born so, too, did the dream of cultural integration become a reality. The half-lost Ireland of the hedge-schools, of the oral tradition and the Irish language, crept into the warmth of Anglo-Irish hospitality. And nowhere did that happen more fruitfully or more triumphantly than among the woods and glades of Coole Park in Co. Galway.

> I have heard the pigeons of the Seven Woods
> Make their faint thunder, and the garden bees
> Hum in the lime-tree flowers; and put away
> The unavailing outcries and the old bitterness
> That empty the heart. I have forgot awhile
> Tara uprooted, and new commonness
> Upon the throne and crying about the streets
> And hanging its paper flowers from post to post,
> Because it is alone of all things happy.
> I am contented for I know that Quiet
> Wanders laughing and eating her wild heart
> Among pigeons and bees, while that Great Archer
> Who but awaits His hour to shoot, still hangs
> A cloudy quiver over Pairc-na-lee.
>
> *In the Seven Woods.* W. B. Yeats.

Augusta Persse, who was to become mistress of that significant demesne at Gort, was born in 1852 at Roxborough House, not far from Coole itself. She had fifteen brothers and sisters but none was quite as remarkable as she. John Butler Yeats's portrait records a spirited, energetic face, almost still that of the young girl who had been relentlessly bored in the stuffy atmosphere of Roxborough House. In 1880, when she was twenty-eight, she married Sir William Gregory of Coole. He was sixty-three.

And boredom, in spite of a happy marriage, would not go away. It was common among spirited women of the time who demanded more of life than hunting and housekeeping, but it rarely cosseted anything even faintly like a literary revival. As a child, when she had a fancy to learn Irish, she was told that it was the language 'of the maids' and not at all suitable for the drawing-room. When her son later expressed the same wish, the widowed Lady Gregory encouraged him, and when he lost interest she continued in his place, using an Irish bible as a textbook. The bible was borrowed from her friend and

Lady Augusta Gregory at Coole Park.
The trees are in their autumn beauty,
The woodland paths are dry,
Under the October twilight the water
Mirrors a still sky;
Under the brimming water among the stones
Are nine-and-fifty swans.

(*The Wild Swans at Coole*: W. B. Yeats)

neighbour, Edward Martyn, a well-to-do Catholic landlord. Some years later, encumbered with the entertaining of a guest on a drearily wet afternoon, Martyn brought him over to Coole.

The guest was W. B. Yeats, known already to Lady Gregory, who politely renewed the acquaintanceship while tea was taken and the talk turned to the theatre. 'I said,' Lady Gregory wrote later, 'it was a pity we had no Irish theatre where such plays could be given. Mr. Yeats said that had always been a dream of his, but he had of late thought it an impossible one. . . . We went on talking and things seemed to grow possible as we talked . . .'

What later became the Abbey Theatre was duly founded, with premises donated by the munificent Miss Horniman of England. The Irish literary revival was under way, and although it is romantic to imagine that its powerhouse was the gracious, if declining, Coole Park there is nevertheless the inescapable fact that the genius of Lady Gregory watched over its birth and later helped to weave its disparate strands together. Her house and gardens became an intellectual rendezvous of a kind unique in the Ireland of that time. One after another the major figures of the new Irish literature were welcomed and given the freedom of the lakes and woods. Under their hostess's insistent eye they carved their initials on her autograph tree, a copper beech that is now the most visited tree in Ireland. 'A blend of the Lord Jesus Christ and Puck,' Sean O'Casey called her, 'a sturdy, stout little figure soberly clad in solemn black made gay with a touch of something white under a long, black silk veil that covered her grey hair and flowed gracefully behind half-way down her back. Her face was a rugged one, hardy as that of a peasant, curiously lit with an odd dignity, and softened with a careless touch of humour in the bright eyes . . .'

She translated many of the old Celtic myths from the ancient vernacular in which they had been recorded. She also became involved in the Gaelic League and the new agricultural co-operatives that were part of the emergent nation. The excitement that had been missing in her life found expression in a nationalism which the people of Ireland, starved of such emotion for so long, were now eagerly lapping up. She, and most of Coole Park's guests, were of the Ascendancy that no longer was, the inheritors of Swift's rasping demand for sense and justice. It is interesting that when the ashes of this upper-class Irish Protestantism had almost ceased to glow they should have ignited so powerful an explosion. Before she died Lady Gregory saw her dream laid out before her while her house at Coole deteriorated, as if both were part of the same pattern of decay and rejuvenation. Yeats wrote:

> Here, traveller, scholar, poet, take your stand
> When all those rooms and passages are gone,
> When nettles wave upon a shapeless mound
> And saplings root among the broken stone,
> And dedicate – eyes bent upon the ground,
> Back turned upon the brightness of the sun
> And all the sensuality of the shade –
> A moment's memory to that laurelled head.

from *Coole Park, 1929.*

Less than ten years later the house was demolished, but since that time its walls have been built up to a height of three feet to indicate the outline of what is now a national shrine. The grounds have been taken over by the Forestry and Wild Life Service, a fate that would surely have pleased the remarkable woman whose own effervescent personality rescued her from what might have been a solidary widowhood of yet more tedium. Her affection for Ireland and for Coole Park became synonymous; in her inspiration landscape and literature had equal parts to play.

Edward Martyn lived only a few miles from Coole Park, in Tulira (or Tullira) Castle. He was an eccentric – as indeed Lady Gregory herself may have seemed to local people, and as her circle of friends most certainly did. When Violet Martin met Yeats she wrote to her cousin Edith that he looked like 'a

Coole House, painting by W. B. Yeats.

starved R.C. curate — in seedy black clothes — with a large black bow at the root of his long naked throat. He is egregiously the poet, murmurs ends of verses to himself with a wild eye, bows over your hand in dark silence, but poet he is, and very interesting indeed, and somehow sympathetic to talk to. . . . He thinks *The Real Charlotte* very big, in the only parts he has read, which are merely quotations in reviews.' A generous opinion in the end, for the cousins tended to be patronized by the literary set: '. . . a great fat oily beast,' Edith had described Oscar Wilde, 'He pretended the most enormous interest'.

Wealth and Catholicism were a combination occasionally to be found in the West of Ireland at that time, and it was one which Martyn shared with George Moore, who lived in Moore Hall in Co. Mayo. The men were cousins and friends, only becoming enemies when Moore's celebrated portrait of Martyn in *Hail and Farewell* inspired Martyn to literary revenge in the last of the plays he wrote. In spite of their religion, both belonged naturally in the twilight of the Protestant Ascendancy, drawing their friends from it even if, like the other figures of the Irish Literary Theatre, they thought in terms of a more purely Irish Ireland than was popular among the Anglo-Irish of less intellectual mould.

In the end, Martyn found the down-to-earth quality that had begun to spread into the plays of the Abbey too much for him, preferring the original literary style he had shared with Yeats. Moore, who had hindered more than helped in his effort to assist Lady Gregory and Yeats to found the theatre, wrote novels set in England after he'd learnt how to play the part of the Great Writer in Paris. He was his own worst enemy, tiresome in all sorts of ways, yet of all the writers who hovered about the Abbey in its infancy he was in several respects the most talented and the most original. His novels are underrated today and his Irish short stories vastly so. *Celibate Lives* contains classics of this especially Irish form; one in particular, *Alfred Nobbs*, will hold its place as a work of genius for as long as the form continues.

Edward Martyn died in 1923, leaving his huge library to the Carmelite nuns and his body to medicine. Perversely, he insisted that when medicine had finished with it the bones should be given a pauper's funeral. George Moore lived for a further ten years, died in London, and left instructions for his ashes to be returned to Co. Mayo, to be placed beneath a cairn near his birthplace at Carra Lough. The burnt-out shell of Moore Hall is still there, another memorial on the shores of the lake.

Lady Gregory was the midwife, but it was Yeats who eventually dominated everything. He came of a family, originally English, which had collected Irish-Norman overtones through marriage with the Butlers. His father, John Butler Yeats, was a painter of considerable merit who moved between London and Dublin in pursuit of portrait commissions. As a result, childhood for his children was unsettled and, for his older son in particular, often so unhappy that it was lightened only by trips to Sligo to stay with uncles and aunts. W. B. Yeats was never to forget the simple ordinariness of the town, or the ways of its people. The narrow streets of Sligo are only a little different from those of other Irish towns, its 'bare houses' unremarkable except when misted with affection. 'Yet their dashed fronts mounting above empty pavements have a kind of dignity in their utilitarianism. They seem to say, "fashion has not made us, nor ever do its caprices pass our sand-cleaned doorsteps."'

Not much, in fact, of the whole county was ever forgotten, the bay where moonlight glossed 'the dim grey sands with light', the waterfall at Glencar, the island in Lough Gill immortalized as Innisfree. It was in childhood that the place had acquired its magic, becoming more than just a haven, more than the ground where the family had its roots. Yeats loved Co. Sligo passionately, and its landscape became the physical presence of the Ireland that stirs his poetry.

Moore Hall, Co. Mayo, birthplace of George Moore, the novelist. Nothing remains but the shell; the interior was burned during the Troubles.

I longed for a sod of earth from some field I knew, something of Sligo to hold in my hand. It was some old race instinct like that of a savage, for we had been brought up to laugh at all display of emotion. Yet it was our mother, who would have thought its display a vulgarity, who kept alive that love. She would spend hours listening to stories or telling stories of the pilots and fishing people of Rosses Point, or of her own Sligo girlhood, and it was always assumed between her and us that Sligo was more beautiful than other places.

from Reveries over Childhood and Youth.

Heartache was soothed in Sligo, the world's weeping held at a distance by its waters and its wild, evenings were full of the linnet's wings. 'Down at Sligo,' Yeats wrote, 'one sees the whole world in a day's walk, every man is a class. It is too small there for minorities.' And on the flat top of Knocknarea a cairn marks, so legend claims, the grave of Queen Medb:

> The wind has bundled up the clouds high over Knocknarea,
> And thrown the thunder on the stones for all that Maeve can·say.
> Angers that are like noisy clouds have set our hearts abeat;
> But we have all bent low and low and kissed the quiet feet
> Of Cathleen, the daughter of Houlihan.

from Red Hanrahan's Song about Ireland. W. B. Yeats.

Yeats became a regular caller at Lissadell, home of the Gore-Booth family, where his nationalism had a considerable effect on the older daughter, Constance, afterwards to become Countess Markiewicz. The Gore-Booths were a cultured Anglo-Irish family who lived stylishly in Co. Sligo and went to London for the Season. Constance rebelled, becoming not only a suffragette and the first woman Member of Parliament at Westminster but also an Irish revolutionary of the briskest kind. Later Yeats wrote about both sisters and about the house, which became yet another Sligo wonder for him.

My father read me some passage out of Walden *and I planned some day to live in a cottage on a little island called Innisfree . . . (Reveries over Childhood and Youth*: W. B. Yeats)

Lissadell House, Co. Sligo, home of the beautiful sisters, Eva and Constance
Gore-Booth.

The light of evening, Lissadell,
Great windows open to the south,
Two girls in silk kimonos, both
Beautiful, one a gazelle.
But a raving autumn shears
Blossom from the summer's wreath;
The older is condemned to death,
Pardoned, drags out lonely years
Conspiring among the ignorant.
I know not what the younger dreams –
Some vague Utopia – and she seems,
When withered old and skeleton-gaunt,
An image of such politics.
Many a time I think to seek
One or the other out and speak
Of that old Georgian mansion, mix
Pictures of the mind, recall
That table and the talk of youth,
Two girls in silk kimonos, both
Beautiful, one a gazelle.

from *In Memory of Eva Gore-Booth and Con Markiewicz*. W. B. Yeats.

But Yeats was also, again and again, drawn back to Coole – and to Vernon Lodge, which was Lady Gregory's seaside house in Co. Clare. Near by, he discovered the ruined abbey of Corcomroe, once known as the abbey of Our Lady of the Fertile Rock. He used it as the setting for his play *The Dreaming of the Bones.*

> I can see
> The Aran Islands, Connemara Hills,
> And Galway in the breaking light; there too
> The enemy has toppled roof and gable,
> And torn the panelling from ancient rooms;
> What generations of old men had known
> Like their own hands, and children wondered at,
> Has boiled a trooper's porridge.
>
> from *The Dreaming of the Bones.* W. B. Yeats.

Yeats had an instinct for places. Almost within hailing distance of Coole, on the Galway–Clare border, he had long admired 'the old square castle, Ballylee . . . and a little mill . . . and old ash trees throwing green shadows upon a little

116

Left: the ruins of Corcomroe Abbey, Co. Clare.

Thoor Ballylee, Yeats's Norman tower near Gort, Co. Galway.

> *An ancient bridge, and a more ancient tower,*
> *A farmhouse that is sheltered by its wall,*
> *An acre of stony ground,*
> *Where the symbolic rose can break in flower . . .*

(*My House*: W. B. Yeats)

river and great stepping-stones.' The blind poet Raftery had written about a beauty whom he called 'the shining flower of Ballylee'. There was also a local witch, long dead, about whom stories were still told. But it was the tranquillity and the twilight atmosphere that gave Thoor Ballylee its real magic for Yeats. He bought it in 1916.

The tower, a fairly Spartan nest for old age – which is what Yeats at first planned – underwent some renovation, 'with old millboards and sea-green slates', and was then dedicated to his wife, a poetic gesture remembered in the inscription which Yeats composed himself and which so excites the cameras of today's tourists. 'And may these characters remain,' he pleaded, 'When all is ruin once again.' It became the Yeatses' holiday house, being more suitable for habitation in the warm summer months. After his death, it deteriorated as he had anticipated, but the dilapidation was arrested when his fame as Ireland's major poet demanded that all he had been close to should be revered.

It was naturally to Sligo that he returned in death, to the hump of Ben Bulben and the grassy slopes beneath it. He sought the companionship of forbears in that landscape, the Pollexfens, the Butlers, the Middletons. He joined them in their Sligo clay.

117

In the poetry of W. B. Yeats — and in the painting of his brother Jack — there is the genius of the artist who is capable of using the parochial to illuminate the human condition. Ireland was their inspiration: Irish legend, Irish landscape, Irish people, Irish places. But neither the poetry nor the painting belongs solely to Ireland today. The sun in Jack Yeats's *And Grania Saw this Sun go Down* is anybody's sun, and Grania, the tempestuous girlfriend of Diarmuid, may be identified as fickle love the world over. *The Man Who Dreamed of Faeryland* is a man in a crowd at Dromahair, but more importantly he is the dreamer who is everywhere.

He stood among a crowd at Dromahair;
His heart hung all upon a silken dress,
And he had known at last some tenderness,
Before earth took him to her stony care;
But when a man poured fish into a pile,
It seemed they raised their little silver heads,
And sang what gold morning or evening sheds
Upon a woven world-forgotten isle,
Where people love beside the ravelled seas;
That Time can never mar a lover's vows
Under that woven changeless roof of boughs:
The singing shook him out of his new ease.

He wandered by the sands of Lissadell;
His mind ran all on money cares and fears,
And he had known at last some prudent years
Before they heaped his grave under the hill;
But while he passed before a plashy place,
A lug-worm with its gray and muddy mouth
Sang that somewhere to north or west or south
There dwelt a gay, exulting, gentle race
Under the golden or the silver skies;
That if a dancer stayed his hungry foot
It seemed the sun and moon were in the fruit:
And at that singing he was no more wise.

He mused beside the well of Scanavin,
He mused upon his mockers: without fail
His sudden vengeance were a country tale,
When earthy night had drunk his body in;
But one small knot-grass growing by the pool
Sang where — unnecessary cruel voice —
Old silence bids its chosen race rejoice,
Whatever ravelled waters rise and fall
Or stormy silver fret the gold of day,

118

Under bare Ben Bulben's head
In Drumcliff churchyard Yeats is laid.
An ancestor was rector there
Long years ago, a church stands near,
By the road an ancient cross.
No marble, no conventional phrase;
On limestone quarried near the spot
By his command these words are cut:
    Cast a cold eye
    On life, on death.
    Horseman, pass by!

      (*Under Ben Bulben*: W. B. Yeats)

And midnight there enfold them like a fleece
And lover there by lover be at peace.
The tale drove his fine angry mood away.

He slept under the hill of Lugnagall;
And might have known at last unhaunted sleep
Under that cold and vapour-turbaned steep,
Now that the earth had taken man and all:
Did not the worms that spired about his bones
Proclaim with that unwearied, reedy cry
That God has laid His fingers on the sky,
That from those fingers glittering summer runs
Upon the dancer by the dreamless wave.
Why should those lovers that no lovers miss
Dream, until God burn Nature with a kiss?
The man has found no comfort in the grave.

     The Man Who Dreamed of Faeryland. W. B. Yeats.

119

A nation without a literature was not fully a nation, Yeats had insisted. The Irish political dream had to find some cultural connection, a reflection of its own nationalism to be teased from the ancient epics, from the poetry and the stories that had survived the determined onslaught of another nation's imperialism. Lady Gregory had gathered and translated some at least of the epics, Yeats himself had given them a modern form and had been influenced by Gaelic verse. It was left to John Millington Synge (1871–1909) to capture the colourful vigour of peasant conversation, an Irishness that could quite easily have been overlooked.

Encouraged by Yeats, Synge discovered an Ireland that no one, a generation before, would have agreed existed. He had been pottering about in Paris, reading Racine and worrying about his perception of French literature. Obedient to Yeats's advice that he should go to the Aran Islands and 'express a life that has never found expression', he forsook the boulevards for the edge of the Atlantic. In his notebooks he describes the stone walls and the little flat fields, smooth with naked rock.

> I have seen nothing so desolate. Grey floods of water were sweeping everywhere upon the limestone, making at times a wild torrent of the road, which twined continually over low hills and cavities in the rock or passed between a few small fields of potatoes or grass hidden away in corners that had shelter. Whenever the cloud lifted I could see the edge of the sea below me on the right, and the naked ridge of the island above me on the other side. Occasionally I passed a lonely chapel or schoolhouse, or a line of stone pillars with crosses above them and inscriptions asking a prayer for the soul of the person they commemorated.

As the wily Yeats had guessed it would, the environment made Synge ravenous with a desire to know more about its people:

> . . . a band of tall girls passed me on their way to Kilronan, and called out to me with humorous wonder, speaking English with a slight foreign intonation that differed a good deal from the brogue of Galway. The rain and cold seemed to have no influence on their vitality, and as they hurried past me with eager laughter and great talking in Gaelic, they left the wet masses of rock more desolate than before.

Everyone talked to Synge. They told him the story of the child who had been found with a wound inflicted on its neck by some supernatural creature. They told him the story of Lucifer as the explanation for the abodeless spirits that work evil wherever they surface. They told him what someone else – miles away and centuries ago – had once told Shakespeare: a complicated rigmarole which was pruned and polished before being incorporated in *The Merchant of Venice*. And naively presented, there was the plot of *Cymbeline*. 'It gave me a strange feeling of wonder to hear this illiterate native of a wet rock in the Atlantic telling a story that is so full of European associations.'

Girls in the Aran Islands, photographed by J. M. Synge.

There were, of course, less familiar tales, and more ordinary ones. Murder loomed large; acts of daring or violence crudely exploded the conventions. Enthralled, Synge listened to the account of the man from the mainland who

killed his father with the blow of a spade when he was in passion, and then fled to this island and threw himself on the mercy of some of the natives with whom he was said to be related. They hid him in a hole – which the old man has shown me – and kept him safe for weeks, though the police came and searched for him, and he could hear their boots grinding on the stones over his head. In spite of a reward which was offered, the island was incorruptible, and after much trouble the man was safely shipped to America.

This impulse to protect the criminal is universal in the west. It seems partly due to the association between justice and the hated English jurisdiction, but more directly to the primitive feeling of these people, who are never criminals yet always capable of crime, that a man will not do wrong unless he is under the influence of a passion which is as irresponsible as a storm on the sea. If a man has killed his father, and is already sick and broken with remorse, they can see no reason why he should be dragged away and killed by the law.

When *The Playboy of the Western World* repeated that same story on the stage of the Abbey Theatre there were riots of denial and disbelief. Where was the

121

Co. Wicklow. Synge walked along these roads and studied the Wicklow people. He himself photographed this tramp (left), possibly the old sailor he describes in his essay *The Vagrants of Wicklow*.

Irishman who would murder his father? Where were the heathen people who would cover up the crime? Had Ireland freed herself only to be maligned and insulted?

Synge was savaged by Dublin, and in a sense by Belfast also, for that city's writers – men like Robert Lynd and Forrest Reid and St John Ervine – had little patience with what they considered to be an exaggerated, eccentric southern style. Ervine went further, stating that the peasant dialect was fraudulent and appearing to suggest that Synge had made it up as he went along. These hard-headed Northerners considered the humorous melancholy of the plays sentimental and obvious. But as time cruelly reveals, it was they who were sentimental. Synge was the realist, and whether the Dublin audiences of 1907 liked it or not, the Ireland that laughed at them from the stage of the Abbey was as real as they were.

Synge wrote about people who were so close to the elements that they could not have lived without that proximity, so close to the seaweed of the strand and the turf of the bogs that those places had become part of them. His vagrants of Wicklow were investigated with the same ruthless curiosity, and put down on paper without either ornamentation or tidying up. And the surrounding landscape arrested his imagination as keenly as the people who stepped out of it. The solitude he experienced recalls Griffin and Banim; nothing had changed in almost a hundred years.

Towards the top of the hill I passed through a narrow gap with high rocks on one side of it and fir trees above them, and a handful of jagged sky filled with extraordinarily brilliant stars. In a few moments I passed out on the brow of the hill that runs behind the Devil's Glen, and smelt the fragrance of the bogs. I mounted again. There was not light enough to show the mountains round me, and the earth seemed to have dwindled away into a mere platform where an astrologer might watch. Among these emotions of the night one cannot wonder that the madhouse is so often named in Wicklow.

Another night is different, gentler, if no less melancholy. What, Synge wonders, has given that 'vague but passionate anguish' to the twilights of Ireland?

... this season particularly when the first touch of autumn is felt in the evening air ... makes me long that the twilight might be eternal. . . . At such moments one regrets every hour that one has lived outside Ireland and every night that one has passed in cities. Twilight and autumn are both full of the suggestion that we connect with death and the ending of earthly vigour, and perhaps in a country like Ireland this moment has an emphasis that is not known elsewhere.

Synge was himself of Co. Wicklow, of Church of Ireland stock that recalls Goldsmith's. His father was a barrister, with property in Co. Galway that was of too modest a nature to make the Synges a landed family. A quiet, delicate man, superficially academic and without the obvious spark displayed by so many figures in the Irish Revival, John Millington Synge was a surprising voice of the people. Yet, more than Yeats or Edward Martyn, more than George Moore, AE, or the host of others who were now establishing for Ireland a place in world literature, Synge was that. Though of the Pale, he belonged outside it. Though a poor relation of the Protestant Ascendancy, he belonged outside it also. Perhaps, indeed, he felt he belonged with the tramps he wrote of, whom he regarded as the wandering aristocracy of the hills and the glens.

But he had just as much respect, of a different kind, for the less restless people of Co. Wicklow who preferred to stay where they were. Like the inhabitants of the Western seaboard, they had been moulded by place and weather and chose to live

for the most part beside old roads and pathways where hardly one man passes in the day, and look out all the year on unbroken barriers of heath. At every season heavy rains fall for often a week at a time, till the thatch drips with water stained to a dull chestnut, and the floor in the cottages seems to be going back to the condition of the bogs near it. Then the clouds break, and there is a night of terrific storm from the south-west – all the larches that survive in these places are bowed and twisted towards the point where the sun rises in June – when the winds come down through the narrow glens with the congested whirl and roar of a torrent, breaking at times for sudden moments of silence that keep up the tension of the mind. At such times the people crouch all night over a few sods of turf, and the dogs howl in the lanes.

In his lonely travels Synge contemplated with wonder what both cottagers and tramps contemplated daily, and probably wished they didn't have to. Every aspect of his surroundings fascinated him. He felt nature for ever closing in.

The fog has come down in places; I am meeting multitudes of hares that run round me at a little distance – looking enormous in the mists – or sit up on their ends against the sky line to watch me going by. When I sit down for a moment the sense of loneliness has no equal. I can hear nothing but the slow running of water and the grouse crowing and chuckling underneath the band of cloud.

On a clear night Synge's Wicklow sky is now lit by the neon of Dublin, and the advancing proximity of the city has drawn some of the mystery from his 'white empty roads winding everywhere'. But there is still, on the right day, the feeling of desolation he describes, and a few wrens singing by a lake can still fill a whole valley with sound. 'All the same I give it ten years,' a Wicklow farmer said recently on the radio. 'In ten years' time old Wicklow will all have disappeared.'

Delightful to be on the Hill of Howth,
very sweet to be above its white sea;
the perfect fertile hill, home of ships,
the vinegrown pleasant warlike peak.
The peak where Finn and Fianna used to be,
the peak where were drinking-horns and cups,
the peak where bold Ó Duinn brought Grainne
one day in stress of pursuit.

(Anonymous, 14th-century (?).
Translated from the Irish by Kenneth Hurlstone Jackson)

Trapped in its neon, Dublin is disappearing also. In its time it has most profitably belonged to the Vikings and the eighteenth century, to politics and business. Trade pitter-pattered along sleepy quays before Georgian development turned a town into a city by decorating it with distinctive skylines, with elegant halldoors, and fanlights and fluted pillars. The nobility of Dublin's squares once mocked the slums of Sean O'Casey (1880–1964); and James Joyce (1882–1941) had to travel to Zürich and Pola and Trieste in order to distill the city's mercurial spirit. Against the odds, Dublin still manages to retain a character that is its own, though parts of it could be anywhere in Europe: the same insurance-company brickwork, the same failure of post-war architecture, motor-cars locked to a standstill. But the past dies hard in these streets and Dubliners themselves supply another continuity – in the timeless quality of their gossip and their old-fashioned turn of phrase.

Joyce and O'Casey were preceded by Shaw (1856–1950), for whom the boyhood journey from Synge Street to St Stephen's Green, every day to school, was one he never forgot because he hated it so. He detested the poverty of Dublin, the dirt, the coarseness, the rough and tumble of its street life. When the Shaw family moved out to Dalkey he enjoyed far more the yellow gorse of Killiney Hill and the lace-curtain orderliness for which he had a secret hankering.

Shaw had been born too soon to be involved very deeply in the Literary Revival. Nothing much was happening from that point of view when he left Ireland in 1876, and he could identify 'no seed of culture' that was particularly native. When he returned to Dublin thirty years later he found it, 'as a tourist', a more charming environment than he remembered. The Abbey put on *The Shewing-up of Blanco Posnet*, which pleased him also. He walked again on Killiney Hill, wondering what it would be like to live in the city's suburban seclusion now. But it was too late. He had made his corner in England and had perceived already that England's bustle and its political debate suited him well. He stayed where he was.

Joyce left Dublin in as grumpy a mood as Shaw, though at a much later date (1904). The Celtic Twilight had suffused the land with a glow about which he remained just a little cool. With Shaw he had in common a Dubliner's wiriness, an urban detachment that did not readily mix with fresh visions of the long ago. Joyce's Dublin is a very different realm from Queen Medb's Cruachan, and in his pages its evocation is very differently arrived at: as eloquently as the city tells the stories of *Dubliners*, it tells Joyce's own.

He was involved with the capital in a way that was totally unlike Yeats's bubbling involvement with Co. Sligo or Synge's curiosity about Wicklow and the West. He stood back to be fascinated – in a dry, cold, almost clinical way. His Dublin is all names and shop-fronts, brass plates and boarding-houses, Mooney's and Findlater's, Pim's and Waterhouse's and Davy Byrne's. Howth was for love-making, the streets for arguing with Oliver St John Gogarty, who also led him towards the Hay Hotel. That famous hostelry derived its name from the hay the horses munched while their masters had their way with the whores it housed. But for Joyce – or Stephen Dedalus – excursions into nighttown were more often solitary:

> It would be a gloomy secret night. After early nightfall the yellow lamps would light up, here and there, the squalid quarter of the brothels. He would follow a devious course up and down the streets, circling always nearer and nearer in a

tremor of fear and joy, until his feet led him suddenly round a dark corner. The whores would be just coming out of their houses making ready for the night, yawning lazily after their sleep and settling the hairpins in their clusters of hair.

from *A Portrait of the Artist as a Young Man.*

That Dublin of the bawds constantly burst its staid Georgian seams. The stench of poverty was lost in the wafting scents of Fresh Nelly and Gertie MacDowell. The heaven of sin was Stephen Dedalus's irresistible enticement:

He wandered up and down the dark slimy streets peering into the gloom of lanes and doorways, listening eagerly for any sound. He moaned to himself like some baffled prowling beast. He wanted to sin with another of his kind, to force another being to sin with him and to exult with her in sin. He felt some dark presence moving irresistibly upon him from the darkness, a presence subtle and murmurous as a flood filling him wholly with itself. Its murmur besieged his ears like the murmur of some multitude in sleep; its subtle streams penetrated his being. His hands clenched convulsively and his teeth set together as he suffered the agony of its penetration. He stretched out his arms in the street to hold fast the frail swooning form that eluded him and incited him: and the cry that he had strangled for so long in his throat issued from his lips. It broke from him like a wail of despair from a hell of sufferers and died in a wail of furious entreaty, a cry for an iniquitous abandonment, a cry which was but the echo of an obscene scrawl which he had read on the oozing wall of a urinal.

He had wandered into a maze of narrow and dirty streets. From the foul laneways he heard bursts of hoarse riot and wrangling and the drawling of drunken singers. He walked onward, undismayed, wondering whether he had strayed into the quarter of the jews. Women and girls dressed in long vivid gowns traversed the street from house to house. They were leisurely and perfumed. A trembling seized him and his eyes grew dim. The yellow gas flames arose before his troubled vision against the vapoury sky, burning as if before an altar. Before the doors and in the lighted halls groups were gathered arrayed as for some rite. He was in another world; he had awakened from a slumber of centuries.

Great cities pile up their period flavours and become a changing amalgam of them all: when Joyce wrote about Dublin, the present he so meticulously reproduced, like a written photograph, was also full of the past. 'When you remember,' he wrote, 'that Dublin has been a capital for thousands of years . . . it seems strange that no artist has given it to the world.'

That is what he set out to do. *Dubliners* was to present the childhood, youth, middle age and public life of the city, to catch its citizens' varying moods and emotions, to expose their mundane predicaments and regrets, often simply to let them talk to one another. *Ulysses* was, apart from everything else, a blueprint from which the city might one day be rebuilt. In fact, unhappily, it has been rebuilt without it.

Grafton Street, Dublin, *c.* 1900.

The grey warm evening of August had descended upon the city, and a mild warm air, a memory of summer, circulated in the streets. The streets, shuttered for the repose of Sunday, swarmed with a gaily coloured crowd. Like illumined pearls the lamps shone from the summits of their tall poles upon the living texture below, which, changing shape and hue unceasingly, sent up into the warm grey evening air an unchanging, unceasing murmur.

Two young men came down the hill of Rutland Square . . .

They were the gallants of the story of that title, Lenehan and Corley, Dublin familiars still easily to be found today. Joyce's people are forever making their way through the city streets; in *An Encounter* the travellers are two small boys.

We walked along the North Strand Road till we came to the Vitriol Works and then turned to the right along the Wharf Road. . . . We came then near the river. We spent a long time walking about the noisy streets flanked by high stone walls,

128

Left: the River Liffey, Dublin. Right: Martello Tower, Dublin, setting for the opening of *Ulysses*.
The cold domed room of the tower waits. Through the barbicans the shafts of light
are moving ever, slowly ever as my feet are sinking, creeping duskward
over the dial floor. (*Ulysses*: James Joyce)

watching the working of cranes and engines and often being shouted at for our immobility by the drivers of groaning carts. It was noon before we reached the quays and, as all the labourers seemed to be eating their lunches, we bought two big currant buns and sat down to eat them on some metal piping beside the river. We pleased ourselves with the spectacle of Dublin's commerce – the barges signalled from far away by their curls of woolly smoke, the brown fishing fleet beyond Ringsend, the big white sailing vessel which was being discharged on the opposite quay.

Dolphin's Barn, Drumcondra, Stoneybatter, Clanbrassil Street Upper, Fishamble, Finglas: the names have a ring to them that echoes the accent of Dubliners. Joyce lived at more than twenty different Dublin addresses before he banished the city to his memory and caused stately, plump Buck Mulligan to bless Dublin Bay from the gunrest of the Sandycove Martello Tower, jewel now of Joycean academe. Braithwaite Street, Brabazon Street, the City Markets, the College of Surgeons, Duke's Lane Lower, Appian Way – slipping by, skulking in the shadows, Joyce is everywhere. Corley's 'fine tart', that sorrowful nameless skivvy, had a place in a house in Baggot Street but after Corley's attentions would have it no more. Mrs Emily Sinico met her death while crossing the line at Sydney Parade railway station; Mr Kernan tasted tea in Crow Street, spelt then with an 'e'. The harpist played the melodies of Tom Moore on the steps of the Kildare Street Club, and out in leafy Chapelizod – immortalized already by Sheridan le Fanu – Dublin's murky old river turned into a woman.

> Ah, but she was the queer old skeowsha anyhow, Anna Livia, trinket-toes! And sure he was the quare old buntz too, Dear Dirty Dumpling, foostherfather of fingalls and dotthergills. Gammer and gaffer we're all their gangsters.
>
> from *Finnegans Wake*.

'Dear Joyce,' wrote Yeats from Coole Park, ' . . . I am very sorry I cannot help you with money. I did my best to get you work as you know, but that is all I can do for you. Yours scy W. B. Yeats.'

'Dear Joyce,' wrote AE, from the editorial sanctuary of the *Irish Homestead*, ' . . . Could you write something simple, rural? livemaking? pathos?, which could be inserted so as not to shock the readers . . . '

Joyce had other ideas, and went on thinking about Dublin. 'I have reproduced none of the attractions of the city,' he later recorded himself. 'I have not reproduced its ingenuous insularity and its hospitality . . . I have not been just to its beauty.' Long before he finished *Dubliners* or had even properly begun it, he set out on his travels. 'Make up a parcel of a toothbrush and powder,' he requested a friend, 'a nail brush, a pair of black boots and any coat and vest you have to spare.' Then he was off, taking the city and Nora Barnacle with him, distancing himself in exile, as many Irish writers have found it necessary to do. He returned only occasionally and then for business purposes: to found a cinema, to pick up samples of the Irish tweeds he hoped to sell to Italians, to argue for the publication of *Dubliners*. In almost all his ventures Dublin let him down.

It let O'Casey down too, and he in turn departed also. For him its remembered landscape was essentially a landscape of people, of features shaped by guile and scrounging, of quick eyes and lips, of dignity preserved through tragedy. Things fell apart, yet there was something left. Pretty it was, to see 'the women scouring their doorsteps; or, possibly, one with a little more money, painting it a bright red or a fair blue; or, in old skirts and blouses, cleaning their windows with rags and paraffin, sometimes exchanging gossip from opposite sides of the street, both busy at their windows, and never once turning to look at one another.'

But beyond the polished windows there was the Dublin which Shaw so loathed and which O'Casey did not forgive the world for permitting. Woven through the drama of *Shadow of a Gunman*, through *The Plough and the Stars* and *Juno and the Paycock*, poverty and penny-pinching tawdriness are made bearable only by the lilt of a city's language.

In Shaw's daintier suburbs the houses were flounced with trimly kept gardens, laurel and privet cooled the heat of the day. At least it cost O'Casey nothing to look, to wander out to the North Circular Road, to gaze upon Phibsboro Church, with its 'Venetian spire thrusting into the deep blue of the sky, looking like a huge spear left behind on the field of one of heaven's battles with Lucifer'. There was the 'dour-bodied Mother of Mercy Hospital' and the 'grimly-grey walls of Mountjoy Jail, where a contingent of Black and Tans smoked the pipe of war, waiting for orders to go forth again and give the Irish another lesson in light and learning'.

O'Casey's Dublin is Ireland in revolution, the drama of the General Post Office and Boland's Mill, of Tommies merry with 'Keep the Home Fires Burning' while the city was ablaze. New heroes were wrapped in the mantles of the folklore martyrs while mothers mourned their sons. The beauty that Yeats called terrible was strewn among the bullets and the victims, but in O'Casey's tenements that poetic description would have drawn forth only a stream of scornful witticisms.

Michael's Lane. O'Casey's Dublin.

From that time on, Dublin became the centre of a literary life that rested comfortably on the laurels recently laid down. George Moore came to live at Number 4 Ely Place. James Stephens became Registrar of the National Gallery. AE held his renowned literary soirées in Rathgar. But many years were to pass before a writer made Dublin as particularly his own as O'Casey and Joyce had. With *At Swim-Two-Birds*, a brilliantly funny successor to *Ulysses*, Flann O'Brien (1912–66) put in his claim just before the Second World War. In this extraordinary fantasy a sense of Dublin transcends streets and buildings to become all things to all men, a playground for the imagination.

> The Circle N is reputed to be the most venerable of Dublin's older ranches. The main building is a gothic structure of red sandstone timbered in the Elizabethan style and supported by corinthian pillars at the posterior. Added as a lean-to at the south gable is the wooden bunk-house, one of the most up-to-date of its kind in the country. It contains three holster-racks, ten gas fires and a spacious dormitory fitted with an ingenious apparatus worked by compressed air by which all verminous beds can be fumigated instantaneously by the mere pressing of a button, the operation occupying only the space of forty seconds. The old Dublin custom of utilizing imported negroid labour for operating the fine electrically-equipped cooking-galley is still observed in this time-hallowed house.

Wheels, in Dublin and in Ireland, had come full circle with a vengeance. *At Swim-Two-Birds* is like nothing so much as *Tristram Shandy*, which Laurence Sterne, a native of Clonmel, had written nearly two hundred years before. O'Brien's Dublin was somewhere to float away from, on stout or wine or as many balls of malt as the constitution could support. Yet like so many other Dublin writers before him – and so many since – there would have been nothing to write about if Dublin had never existed. There is a quality about the city and about its literature that defies precise definition, beyond saying that they are unique and uniquely belong together.

> Old elms, open and half hollow, which were planted to be conduits for water in days before cast-iron or earthenware could be made, gauntly stand in their decay, more sinned against than sinning, and shelter by night the fugitive loves of a city. . . . The path is lovely because it runs beside the long water over-arched by bridges of cut stone which complete their ellipse by reflexion in the calm water.
> from *As I was Going Down Sackville Street*. Oliver St John Gogarty (1878–1957).

Trees and water for Gogarty; the poet Padraic Colum (1881–1972) writes of Dublin roads and the 'high walls to the left and right'. Such noble stone barriers, often now half tumbled down, are a feature of Irish landscape in both town and country. Mostly they are stark except for the ivy that occasionally clothes them or tugs their masonry apart, but Padraic Colum has noticed:

Stone walls, Co. Kerry.

> Over old walls the Laburnums
>   hang cones of fire;
> Laburnums that grow out of old
>   mould in gardens.

from Laburnums.

These walls of Ireland had safely fenced in the Edgeworths and the Herberts and the Brownes, but nothing was quite the same now, after the early 1920s, and never was to be again. The art of the infant nation had reached out, beyond the little pales and into the parklands, weaving together threads that had not before belonged in the same pattern. And the new Ireland, as if not quite satisfied with poetry and drama, had found already a particular form of fiction to match its newness. When the modern short story arrived on the literary horizon the Irish grabbed it.

All over Europe there had, of course, been the long tradition of the story in its antique form. It harked back to the Jatakas, which were narrations that came from the East, illustrating the teaching of Buddha. Within the oral tradition that had lingered so in Ireland, certain refinements had taken place and there were local rules and conventions, including a sharp division between the tale which dealt in the wonders of some distant world and the one which was more closely related to personal experience. But whichever form he relied upon, the storyteller was reverently regarded, a man of magic and of thrall because of the riches of his tongue. For longer than anywhere else in Europe a straggle of such storytellers survived, feeding and shaping the peasant imagination. With Mass and hedge-school, the ceremonial tale-telling provided the excitement of social intercourse for lonely cottagers; and it lay as close as the land itself to the essence of daily life. The fairy-stories of Donegal were heard beneath the shadow of Slieve League and Slieve Snaght, to the wail of the Atlantic.

Nancy and Shamus were man and wife, and they lived all alone together for forty years; but at length a good-for-nothing streel of a fellow named Rory, who lived close by, thought what a fine thing it would be if Shamus would die, and he could marry Nancy, and get the house, farm, and all the stock. So he up and said to Nancy:

'What a pity it is for such a fine-looking woman as you to be bothered with that ould, complainin', good-for-nothing crony of a man that's as full of pains and aches as an egg's full of meat. If you were free of him the morrow, the finest and handsomest young man in the parish would be proud to have you for a wife.'

At first Nancy used to laugh at this; but at last, when he kept on at it, it began to prey on Nancy's mind, and she said to young Rory one day: 'I don't believe a word of what you say. Who would take me if Shamus was buried the morra?'

'Why,' says Rory, 'you'd have the pick of the parish. I'd take you myself.'

'Is that true?' says Nancy.

'I pledge you my word,' says Rory, 'I would.'

'Oh, well, even if you would yourself,' says Nancy, 'Shamus won't be buried to-morrow, or maybe, God help me, for ten years to come yet.'

'You've all that in your own hands,' says Rory.

'How's that?' says Nancy.

'Why, you can kill him off,' says Rory.

'I wouldn't have the ould crature's blood on my head,' says Nancy.

'Neither you need,' says Rory.

from *Donegal Fairy Stories*. Collected and told by Seumas MacManus.

The transformation, when it came, was thorough. As an expression of modernity, the short story of this century is utterly different from everything that preceded it. In Russia Chekhov had turned the antique inside out; Joyce, in Ireland, did the same. The great Victorian novel which had passed Ireland by was at last to be challenged by the art of the glimpse, by a form that is the antithesis of the nineteenth-century literary extravaganzas. The modern short story deals in moments and subtleties and shadows of grey. It tells as little as it dares. It teases in a way that, still today, delights the Irish sensibility and the Irish mind. It suits the Irish mood.

Graveyard in Co. Wicklow reflects the atmosphere of Cloon na Morav in
Seumas O'Kelly's story, *The Weaver's Grave.*

The energy that might have gone into the native novel, had there been the
complacency of a rich Irish society to be punctured by the skilful thrusts of a
Dickens or a George Eliot, went instead, and vigorously, into a native version
of the new form. Even so, nothing happened quickly; the traditional tale-
bearers did not, overnight, become silent. But in the stories that were now
gaining ground the hero figures of the past had little part to play: the Irish
twentieth century was the territory of the underdog, what Frank O'Connor
was to call 'small men' (a territory that has increasingly been shared with hard-
done-by women). The novel had already seized upon the heroics and the meaty
plot patterns that for so long had distinguished the fiction of the world's myths.
In Ireland, as elsewhere, the modern short story grew out of what remained.

In 1919 Seumas O'Kelly published *The Weaver's Grave*, a remarkable tale
that has since become a classic. It has often been pointed out that Susanna and
the Elders in the Apocrypha is a unified short story, an antique example of the
modern art: *The Weaver's Grave* is a reversal of that, a modern expression of the
Irish antique. In it a graveyard, Cloon na Morav, is translated from the Irish as
the Meadow of the Dead, and the story centres round the search for the burial
plot that is the final resting-place of Mortimer Hehir the weaver:

No obituary notice in the place was complete; all were either wholly or partially eaten up by the teeth of time. The monuments that had made a stout battle for existence were pathetic in their futility. The vanity of the fashionable of dim ages made one weep. Who on earth could have brought in the white marble slab to Cloon na Morav? It had grown green with shame. Perhaps the lettering, once readable upon it, had been conscientiously picked out in gold. The shrieking winds and the fierce rains of the hills alone could tell. Plain heavy stones, their shoulders rounded with a chisel, presumably to give them some off-handed resemblance to humanity, now swooned at fantastic angles from their settings, as if the people to whose memory they had been dedicated had shouldered them away as an impertinence. Other slabs lay in fragments on the ground, filling the mind with thoughts of Moses descending from Mount Sinai and, waxing angry at sight of his followers dancing about false gods, casting the stone tables containing the Commandments to the ground, breaking them in pieces – the most tragic destruction of a first edition that the world has known. Still other heavy square dark slabs, surely creatures of a pagan imagination, were laid flat down on numerous short legs, looking sometimes like representations of monstrous black cockroaches, and again like tables at which the guests of Cloon na Morav might sit down, goblin-like, in the moon-light, when nobody was looking.

As a long-winded cottage anecdote, *The Weaver's Grave* is the kind of set piece that had been repeated for generations, but O'Kelly quite ingeniously imbued it with freshness and lent it a colloquial, contemporary wit. He kept it far shorter than it might have been, resisting the many detours and peregrinations that would hitherto have been an essential element. The people it tells of, and the spirit of Cloon na Morav, have been in Ireland for as long as we know about: O'Kelly persuades us that they still are.

No writer could perhaps be less like Seumas O'Kelly than Elizabeth Bowen. Born humbly in Loughrea in Co. Galway in 1880, O'Kelly became a reporter on a local newspaper and was later involved in the revolutionary movement. Elizabeth Bowen (1899–1973) was the daughter of Henry Cole Bowen of Bowenscourt, Co. Cork. She was educated in England and at Trinity in Dublin, and was instinctively Anglo-Irish in outlook and in her understanding of Irish people. In one sense she belongs with Somerville and Ross – though as the authors of *The Real Charlotte* rather than of the RM stories. Her background, like theirs, was the big house, Irish servants, English friends. Her family had been at Bowenscourt since Cromwell's time.

It has been, even still is, popular to suggest that Somerville and Ross and Elizabeth Bowen were somehow not quite Irish, not properly or dedicatedly so. This view, while understandable, is a little glib. These three writers, because of a shared accident of birth, saw the Ireland of William Carleton and later of Seumas O'Kelly from the same kind of distance as the one Joyce had to create for himself in order to dispel a certain claustrophobia. Synge and Yeats sought to reduce such a distance; Elizabeth Bowen simply accepted it. She did not patronize, but looked sideways rather than down; and her affection for places and their people remains as the throb of vitality in all she wrote. Her own particular Ireland possessed her.

> It was Sarah who saw the others ahead on the blond stubble, who knew them, knew what they were to each other, knew their names and knew her own. It was she who felt the stubble under her feet, and who heard it give beneath the tread of the others a continuous different more distant soft stiff scrunch. The field and all these outlying fields in view knew as Sarah knew that they were Papa's. The harvest had been good and was now in: he was satisfied . . .
>
> from *The Happy Autumn Fields*. Elizabeth Bowen.

Elizabeth Bowen writes from within both the hearts and the imaginations of her characters. What they so vividly think and see we think and see ourselves. The leisurely afternoon walk continues:

> They walked inside a continous stuffy sound, but left silence behind them. Behind them, rooks that had risen and circled, sun striking blue from their blue-black wings, planed one by one to the earth and settled to peck again.

Elizabeth Bowen's novels are highly regarded, but in my own estimation it is her stories that carry her art to its height (as, I believe, Joyce's do for his). She understood the short story very precisely, 'a matter of vision, rather than of feeling'. It intrigued her as a new species suddenly appearing in the Bowenscourt gardens might, 'a young art, a child of this century'. And in passing, sketching in a background, no one has as economically and as surely registered the Anglo-Irish landscape of that time:

> The Castle was built on high ground, commanding the estuary; a steep hill, with trees, continued above it. On fine days the view was remarkable, of almost Italian brilliance, with that constant reflection up from the water that even now prolonged the too-long day. Now, in continuous evening rain, the winding wooded line of the further shore could be seen and, nearer the windows, a smothered island with the stump of a watch-tower. Where the Castle stood, a higher tower had answered the island's. Later a keep, then wings, had been added: now the fine peaceful residence had French windows opening on to the terrace. Invasions from the water would henceforth be social, perhaps amorous. On the slope down from the terrace trees began again . . .
>
> from *Her Table Spread*. Elizabeth Bowen.

The house at Bowenscourt, like Coole, no longer exists. Sold in 1959, it was pulled down for the value of the lead in its roof. But not far away, in the small Protestant graveyard at Farahy, Elizabeth Bowen is buried where she wished to be, in an undramatic part of Co. Cork. She is far from the estuary of which so often she wrote, but it is still haunted by her voice.

Mist lay over the estuary, over the terrace, over the hollows of the gummy, sub-tropical garden of the hotel. Now and then a soft, sucking sigh came from the water, as though someone were turning over in his sleep. At the head of the steps down to the boathouse, a patch of hydrangeas still flowered and rotted, though it was December. It was now six o'clock, dark – chinks of light from the hotel lay yellow and blurred on the density. The mist's muffling silence could be everywhere felt. Light from the double glass doors fell down the damp steps. At the head of the steps the cast-iron standard lamps were unlit.

from *A Love Story*. Elizabeth Bowen.

Of Cork also was Daniel Corkery, of an only slightly older generation than Elizabeth Bowen, born in the city in 1878. As an academic, he wrote of 'the hidden Ireland', the Gaelic voice that had never been quite silenced. He also wrote short stories, which more than any fiction of this time dwell upon the harshness of the land as experienced by those who work it. Not for Corkery the splendid sweep of countryside or coast, but clay and rocks and roots.

It is a stony land. The name of it, Kilclaw, might mean either the Stone Church or the Stony Wood. Nobody now knows which. The woods were felled some hundreds of years ago; but felling the trees had not been sufficient, for, that done, even the roughest kind of tillage was not yet possible until the little patches first marked out for it had been cleared of the largest of the stones embedded in them. The roots of them were found to be tougher than those of the wild ash, the mountain fir, or the oak. Yet removed they were, dragged to the sides of the little fields, however they managed it, crop upon crop of them, year after year, decade after decade, century after century, until the stone mounds that now enclose the little patches of wheat or oats or potatoes take up as much, if not more, of the ground than the croppings within them. The boulders earliest removed were huge, huger than would now appear, for their bases once again are hidden deep in the ground. Halfway up their flanks, sometimes all the way, they are clothed with brown and silvery mosses, or with innumerable layers of the tiniest fern.

from *The Stones*.

Belonging to that same culture, sharing the same inspirational instinct, is the gallery of native short-story writers which subsequently kept Ireland on the literary map. Liam O'Flaherty, born in 1896 in the Aran Islands, may well have been one of those islanders who, as a child, had observed with wonder the note-taking J. M. Synge as he made his way from cottage to cottage. As O'Casey's people do in Dublin, so O'Flaherty's become part of his Aran landscape:

Two old women were sitting on the rocks that lay in a great uneven wall along the seashore beyond the village of Rundangan. There were knitting. Their red petticoats formed the only patch of colour among the grey crags about them and behind them. In front of them stretched the sea, blue and calm. It sparkled far out where the sun was shining on it. The sky was blue and empty and the winds were

Estuary of the River Lee, Co. Cork.

silent. The only noise came from the sea, near the shore, where it was just low tide. The water babbled and flopped along the seaweed on the low rocks that lay afar out, black strips of rocks with red seaweed growing on them. It was a spring evening and the air was warm and fresh, as if it had just been sprinkled with eau de cologne or something. The old women were talking in low voices sleepily as they knitted woollen stockings. 'Ah yes', said one of them called Big Bridget Conlon, an old woman of seventy, a woman of great size and strength, with big square jaws like a man, high cheekbones, red complexion and wistful blue eyes that always seemed to be in mourning about something.

Continuing that story, *The Landing*, the idyll is snatched away, as so often it is in Irish literature:

People came running down to the beach from the village as the storm grew in intensity. They gathered together on the wall of boulders with the two old women. Soon there was a cluster of red petticoats and heads hooded in little black shawls, while the men stood about talking anxiously and looking out to sea towards the west. The sea was getting rougher with every wave that broke along the rocky beach. It began to growl and toss about and make noises as if monstrous teeth were being ground. It became alive and spoke with a multitude of different yells that inspired the listeners with horror and hypnotised them into feeling mad with the sea. Their faces set in a deep frown and their eyes had a distant fiery look in them. They shouted when they spoke to one another. Each contradicted the other. They swore angrily. They strutted about on the boulders with their hands behind their backs, looking at the sea suspiciously as if they thought it was going to rush up each minute and devour them.

As terror mounts, the islanders' courage seems like another aspect of the elements that rage about them. Savaged, crushed by fear, humanity staggers to make an effort:

The boat, the crew, the men on the beach, the women on the boulder were all mingled together for a wild moment in a common contempt of danger. For a moment their cries surmounted the sound of the wind and sea. It was the defiance of humanity hurled in the face of merciless nature. And then again there was a strained pause. The noise of voices vanished suddenly and silence came.

On the back of a wave the boat came riding in, the oars stretched out, their points tipping the water. Then the oars dipped. There was a creak, a splash, a rushing sound, a panting of frightened breath, a hurried mumble of excited voices rose from the men on the beach. The men on the beach waited in two lines with clasped hands. The foremost men were up to their waist in water. The boat rushed in between the two lines. They seized the boat. The wave passed over their heads. There was a wild shriek and then confusion. The boat and the foremost men were covered by the wave. Then the wave receded. The boat and the crew and the men holding the boat were left on the rock, clinging to the rock and to one another, like a dragged dog clings to the earth.

The welcome return of the fishing boats, Aran Islands.

O'Flaherty is full of images, swift, dashing little pictures that hang in the mind. But the evocation of place, the precise nature of environment so important to O'Kelly and Elizabeth Bowen, inspires in O'Flaherty a different technique. The nature of events and the nature of people are what matter most and must be given their head as soon as possible. Many Irish writers subsequently adopted the O'Flaherty model and with some notable exceptions the short story in Ireland has ever since been in a hurry. There is, for example, an anecdotal quality about the writing of Frank O'Connor that dictates both pace and content. His landscape strikes an urban, no-nonsense note and even in the heart of the country there's a sedate domesticity that is not lingered over.

> The house was on top of a hill, and behind it rose the mountainside, studded with rocks. There were trees about it, and in front a long garden with a hedge of fuchsia, at one side of which ran a stream. There were four or five apple trees, and beside the kitchen garden were a few flower beds with a profusion of tall snapdragon, yellow, red and white.
>
> from *There is a Lone House*.

But O'Connor, at will, can easily find another mood, even if he does not choose to do so very often:

> It was drawing on to dusk. Shadow was creeping up the mountain. First light faded from the sea, then from the rocks, then from the roadway and the fields. Soon it

would dwindle from the bog; everything there would fill with rich colour and the long channels of dark bogwater would burn like mirrors between the purple walls of turf. Behind each of the channels was ranged a file of turf stacks, black sods heaped to dry and looking like great pine cones.

from The Storyteller.

Sean O'Faolain goes about things differently. He stalks his people down with a ruthless exactitude that is later matched when he supplies the scenery that complements them.

So then, a dusky Sunday afternoon in Bray at a quarter to five o'clock, lighting up time at five fifteen, November 1st. All Souls' Eve, dedicated to the suffering souls in Purgatory. Bertie Bolger, bachelor, aged forty-one or so, tubby, ruddy, greying, well-known as a dealer in antiques, less well-known as a conflator thereof, walking briskly along the seafront, head up to the damp breezes, turns smartly into the lounge of the Imperial Hotel for a hot toddy, singing in a soldierly basso 'my breast expanding to the ball.'

from An Inside Outside Complex.

On Bertie Bolger's mind is a 'twentieth-century Buhl cabinet' which he hopes, somehow, to transform into one that 'might plausibly be attributed to the original M. Boulle'. Because of his preoccupation he has failed, on his walk to the Imperial Hotel, to observe some of the wonders of Bray:

. . . either the red gasometer by the harbour inflated to its winter zenith, or the haybarn beside the dairy beyond the gasometer packed with cubes of hay, or the fuel yard, facing the haybarn, beside the dairy beyond the gasometer, heavily stocked with mountainettes of coal, or the many vacancy signs in the lodging houses along the seafront, or the hoardings on the pagoda below the promenade where his mother, God rest her, had once told him he had been wheeled as a coiffed baby in a white pram to hear Mike Nono singing 'I do liuke to be besiude the seasiude, I do liuke to be besiude the sea,' or, most affectingly of all, if he had only heeded them, the exquisite, dying leaves of the hydrangeas in the public gardens, pale green, pale yellow, frost white, spiking the air above once purple petals that now clink greyly in the breeze like tiny seashells.

A good story economically peels off surfaces. In *The Lost Child* Mary Lavin finds a chilly depth beneath.

They had gone to Achill on one of their week-end trips, and Iris had gone with them. They were staying in a small hotel close to the shore, and they had gone for a stroll along Dugort Strand after putting the children to bed. As they walked along the shore they had to pick their steps, because the tufty shore-grass was dotted with half-concealed stones and they could easily trip and twist an ankle. Suddenly Iris stopped.

'I thought the rocks along here were all part of a natural formation,' she said, 'but look – surely there is some attempt at pattern to this?'

Seafront at Bray, Co. Wicklow.

They were, in fact, walking on the graves of unbaptized infants, ground known locally as Cillin na Leanbh, the Cemetery of the Children. In spite of the recurring accent on solitariness that echoes through Irish literature, you can never count on being entirely alone in Ireland's empty places. And beneath those peeled-off surfaces nothing is quite what you might expect.

The landscape of the short story – whether it's Irish or not – is rather like that of Impressionist painting. Background smudges are never meaningless; what appears to be doodling is vital information. Michael McLaverty (b. 1907), doyen of the form in Ulster, punctuates with unhurried images, as the leisurely O'Faolain does, but in the end is as economic as O'Connor.

> 'Way up, girl,' he shouted to the mare, 'way up, Maggie!' and his veins swelled on his arms as he leant on the handles. The breeze blowing up from the sea, the cold smell of the broken clay, and the soft hizzing noise of the plough, all soothed his mind and stirred him to new life.
>
> As the day advanced the sun rose higher, but there was little heat from it, and frosty vapours still lingered about the rockheads and about the sparse hills. But slowly over the little field horse and plough still moved, moved like timeless creatures of the earth, while alongside their shadows followed on the clay. Overhead and behind swarmed the gulls, screeching and darting for the worms, their flitting shadows falling coolly on Paddy's neck and on the back of the mare.
>
> from *The White Mare*. Michael McLaverty.

McLaverty's tidily ploughed landscape recalls George Moore, whose collection of stories, symbolically entitled *The Untilled Field*, drew attention to the infancy of the form a long time before Elizabeth Bowen did. Moore wrote these stories 'out of no desire of self-expression, but in the hope of furnishing the young Irish of the future with models'. He would assuredly have seen McLaverty and O'Faolain and Mary Lavin as three of these. Ireland's most renowned expert on the modern short story, David Marcus, agrees that Moore was indeed its father. He offers Somerville and Ross as the mother. No literary

143

union, he argues, 'could have been more fruitful of promise, for father and mother emerged from the two widely-opposed cultures (Catholic and Native/Protestant or Anglo, and settler) which had become the constituents of the Irish family'. The conjunction would have pleased Maria Edgeworth in her concern about the fragmentation of Irish culture. So would Moore's *The Exile*, which includes a variation on a familiar dirge.

> The mare trotted gleefully; soft clouds curled over the low horizon far away, and the sky was blue overhead; and the poor country was very beautiful in the still autumn weather, only it was empty. He passed two or three fine houses that the gentry had left to caretakers long ago. The fences were gone, cattle strayed through the woods, the drains were choked with weeds, the stagnant water was spreading out into the fields . . .

In *The Wild Goose*, drawn again towards landscape and the appearance of things, he makes a Moore-ish point.

> . . . And he began to give his reasons for preferring the valley of the Liffey to the plains of Meath, saying that no landscape was altogether sympathetic to him without a river in it. As he had already said he was not a fisherman, she failed to understand, and she was not less puzzled by the remark that whereas County Meath was all meat, County Dublin was all milk . . .

Blarney Lane, Cork.
My memories begin in Blarney Street, which we called Blarney Lane because it follows the track of an old lane from Cork to Blarney. It begins at the foot of Shandon Street, near the riverbank, in sordidness, and ascends the hill to something like squalor. (An Only Child: Frank O'Connor)

The Road to Brightcity

JOURNEY THROUGH Ireland today and poets or storytellers guide you. So do Giraldus Cambrensis, the Halls, and many another enthusiastic visitor who observed the environment with a friendly foreign eye. You can travel more lightly if you wish, but while the landscape of literature remains it's pleasant to have company on a last Grand Tour.

Bells are booming down the bohreens,
    White the mist along the grass.
Now the Julias, Maeves and Maureens
    Move between the fields to Mass.
Twisted trees of small green apple
Guard the decent whitewashed chapel,
Gilded gates and doorway grained
Pointed windows richly stained
    With many-coloured Munich glass.

See the black-shawled congregations
    On the broidered vestment gaze
Murmur past the painted stations
    As Thy Sacred Heart displays
Lush Kildare of scented meadows,
Roscommon, thin in ash-tree shadows,
And Westmeath the lake-reflected,
Spreading Leix the hill-protected,
    Kneeling all in silver haze?

In yews and woodbine, walls and guelder,
    Nettle-deep the faithful rest,
Winding leagues of flowering elder,
    Sycamore with ivy dressed,
Ruins in demesnes deserted,
Bog-surrounded bramble-skirted —
Townlands rich or townlands mean as
These, oh, counties of them screen us
    In the Kingdom of the West.

Stony seaboard, far and foreign,
    Stony hills poured over space,
Stony outcrop of the Burren,
    Stones in every fertile place,

Little fields with boulders dotted,
Grey-stone shoulders saffron-spotted,
Stone-walled cabins thatched with reeds,
Where a Stone Age people breeds
 The last of Europe's stone age race.

Has it held, the warm June weather?
 Draining shallow sea-pools dry,
When we bicycled together
 Down the bohreens fuchsia-high.
Till there rose, abrupt and lonely,
A ruined abbey, chancel only,
Lichen-crusted, time-befriended,
Soared the arches, splayed and splendid,
 Romanesque against the sky.

There in pinnacled protection,
 One extinguished family waits
A Church of Ireland resurrection
 By the broken, rusty gates.
Sheepswool, straw and droppings cover,
Graves of spinster, rake and lover,
Whose fantastic mausoleum
Sings its own seablown Te Deum,
 In and out the slipping slates.

Ireland with Emily. John Betjeman (b. 1906).

It is a far cry from John Betjeman to his contemporary, Máirtín Ó Cadhain, (1906–70) one of whose stories, *The Road to Brightcity*, suggests in its title a landscape in which the present has at last caught up with Ireland's determined past. Eoghan Ó Tuairisc, translating the Irish of Ó Cadhain, points out that Ó Cadhain's people are 'survivors, remnants of a Celtic civilisation that has been pushed ever farther towards the western seaboard by succeeding waves of English-speaking peoples. They have lost everything; forgotten by history, and still sunk in a serf-like medieval economy, they are barely clinging to life on bog, stony garth, mountain pasture and shore.' It is a very familiar Irish tale, but in the new Ireland of the twentieth century Ó Cadhain's people and their language can at least belong – if the sacrifice is not too great.

The fog was being rolled and thinned out and dragged by a freshening wind in grey diminishing strips to the edge of the Plain. As far as her eye could see, nothing but immense flat fields, no stones, no rock-heaps, and every foot of fencing as straight as a fishing-line except where they were submerged in winter flooding. Here and there a stand of trees, a thicket, down below her a few outcrops of bedrock like knots in a deal table that had been bleached and scoured. The spot where she stood was the most airy hill of all the dull rich expanse. The houses were not strung together here,

Brightcity, from North Great George's Street, Dublin.

the nearest wavering thread of smoke seemed to her a mile away. . . . Like all the surrounding countryside her new house had a certain stupid arrogance, it reminded her of the smug smile of a shopkeeper examining his bankbook. Boasting to her face that it was no mushroom growth but a part of the everlasting. She knew it was a 'warm' house. She knew her father wouldn't have set her there if it wasn't, in view of her dowry and all the well-heeled upstarts he had refused on her behalf. She shivered to think that from now on she would be simply one of the conveniences among the conveniences of this house.

Here there was no barrier of mountain and sea to restrain a rambling foot or limit a wandering imagination. Nothing but the smooth monotonous Plain to absorb one's yearnings and privacies and weave them into the one drab undifferentiated fabric, as each individual drop, whatever its shade, whatever its nature before being engulfed in the womb of it, the ocean transmutes into its own grey phantom face. From now on whatever contact she'd have with home would be only a thin thread in this closcknit stuff.

from *The Hare-Lip*. Máirtín Ó Cadhain.

Ó Cadhain's Brightcity glimmers all over the country now, as inevitably it must. Ireland's cities finger their way into once remote hills, suburban development consuming villages and fields. Beyond the fluorescent shopping-centres and wastelands of grey cement, motorcycles scramble through heather and boglands, over scree and rockface. Television transmitters bedeck the peaks. Pylons stride.

Yet nothing can destroy the Ireland of its writers. Yeats's bare Ben Bulben, his Cummen Strand, his Clooth-na-Bare, are there for ever now. So is the faded glory of Kilcash, and Mangan's vision of Connacht. So is James Joyce by the seaside.

> Turning, he scanned the shore south, his feet sinking again slowly in new sockets. The cold domed room of the tower waits. Through the barbicans the shafts of light are moving ever, slowly ever as my feet are sinking, creeping duskward over the dial floor. Blue dusk, nightfall, deep blue night. In the darkness of the dome they wait, their pushedback chairs, my obelisk valise, around a board of abandoned platters. Who to clear it? He has the key. I will not sleep there when this night comes. A shut door of a silent tower entombing their blind bodies, the panthersahib and his pointer. Call: no answer. He lifted his feet up from the suck and turned back by the mole of boulders. Take all, keep all. My soul walks with me, form of forms. So in the moon's midwatches I pace the path above the rocks, in sable silvered, hearing Elsinore's tempting flood.
>   The flood is following me. I can watch it flow past from here. Get back then by the Poolbeg road to the strand there. He climbed over the sedge and eely oarweeds and sat on a stool of rock, resting his ashplant in a grike.
>   A bloated carcass of a dog lay lolled on bladderwrack. Before him the gunwale of a boat, sunk in sand. *Un coche ensablé*, Louis Veuillot called Gautier's prose. These heavy sands are language tide and wind have silted here. And there, the stoneheaps of dead builders, a warren of weasel rats. Hide gold there. Try it. You have some. Sands and stones. Heavy of the past. Sir Lout's toys. Mind you don't get one bang on the ear. I'm the bloody well gigant rolls all them bloody well boulders, bones for my steppingstones. Feefawfum. I zmellz de bloodz odz an Iridzman.
>
> from *Ulysses*.

Nor can anything destroy the story of history, or the saints and scholars who have left behind their voices. Journey through Ireland today and you'll find their echoes, each in its landscape.

Kildare (church of the oak) is St Brigid territory, she who, according to the *Book of Lismore*, never washed her hands or her feet or her head in the presence of other people. She never looked at the face of a man, she never spoke without blushing. Dove among birds, vine among trees, sun among stars, she was a 'consecrated casket for keeping Christ's body and blood, a temple of God'. The story is told that she sat one early morning with Sister Dara, a nun who was blind, and prayed that Dara might share with her, just for an hour or so, the beauty of the Kildare landscape. Her prayer was granted and for the first time in

Above: *And Grania Saw this Sun Go Down*, painting by Jack B. Yeats.

Below. *My road ran round an immense valley of magnificent rich turf bog, with mountains all around, and bowls where hidden lakes were lying bitten out of the cliffs. (In West Kerry*: J. M. Synge)

her life Dara saw the sun rise from behind the Wicklow mountains. Far and near, on the mountains and the trees, on dewy grass and flowers, the pale morning light fell so marvellously and so enhanced the natural beauty that Dara asked her abbess to return her to darkness because her image of God was clouded by this surfeit of visible delight. Which St Brigid meekly did.

In the heart of those Wicklow mountains that same dawn would have glittered on the Avonmore and the Avonbeg, the rivers which meet at Avoca. 'There is not in this wide world,' wrote Tom Moore of the melodies (1779–1852), 'a valley so sweet.' The beauty spot, like many famous beauty spots, hasn't worn all that well, and Moore's verses may not be to everyone's taste. But place and poesy go together like bread and butter, a great deal of which they have between them earned over the years.

> Sweet vale of Avoca! how calm could I rest
> In thy bosom of shade, with the friends I love best,
> Where the storms that we feel in this cold world should cease,
> And our hearts, like thy waters, be mingled in peace.
>
> from *The Meeting of the Waters.*

Oliver St John Gogarty liked to look at Ireland from an aeroplane, Somerville and Ross from a governess cart, Frank O'Connor from a bicycle. Austin Clarke (1896–1974) favoured motoring.

> Pleasant, my Nora, on a May morning to drive
> Along the roads of Ireland, going south,
> See Wicklow hilling from car window, down
> And pinewood, buttercupping grass, field-wire,
> The shelves of hawthorn, konker bud on chestnut
> Bulging with sun-shadowings, brook-lime,
> The yellow iris-curl, flower o' the cress
> And Slaney gliding around a sandy nook
> Through flaggeries into the narrower falls,
> Beyond the mills with rusty flange, cogwheel
> And moss of the sluice, hear the jackdawing,
> Yet sad to speed from the inn, along the bogland
> Where State machines are cutting turf for miles
> That furnaces may stop the centuries
> Of turbary, put out an ancient fire.
> Hardly a living soul upon these roads:
> Both young and old hasten to quit the dung,
> The chicken-run, lean-to, sty, thistle blow
> Of fields once measured by buckshot, midnight bung.

Dugort, Achill Island, resting ground for dead infants.

Foreign factories in towns employ
Chattering girls: few levers for a boy.

Pleasant to climb the Rock of Dunamace,
A goat upon a crag, a falcon swerving
Above: heraldic shield of air, chevroned
With brown and *or*: later the rounded walls
And bastion were raised beside the squat
Keep: they could bounce away the cannon balls.
The culdees knew each drumlin, sun-thatched spot,
By rising road, fern-corner, come to Wolf Hill:
Men working underground, tap anthracite.
Stacks are shed-high. The heatherland is chill.
That earth is black except for a blue-white image
Seen far, a statue of the Blessed Virgin
Beside the road, a solitary hymn
To a great owner. Beneath the pious verge
Of the mine-hill is his public-house, his sign –
The Swan, beside a holy statuette:
Nearby his factory with store of drain-pipes,
Trim row by row, a Sacred Heart beset
By glass of shrine and on the outer wall
Behold a plaque in loving memory
Of Joseph Fleming, Irish patriot,
Industrialist and good employer. Night-stealing,
He fought the English, ready with rifle shot
To serve his country.
                              Higher still
                                        Pleasant,
My love, upon Mount Leinster, passing the spruce,
Fir, pine plantations, as a red-brown pheasant
Comes bustling up from heather, bends the juicy
Grass-stalk, to scan the middle plain below,
A map of cloud, the fields of beetroot penned;
Dividing sea.

                              Signpost to Kilkenny:
The Georgian almshouses, tree-pent College
Where Congreve, Swift, had learned about addition,
The passage steps between the danks of wall,
Martins high up at the city bridge,
Swallows, their black-and-white playing at tig.

                              from *Beyond the Pale.*

The River Nore, by Inistioge, Co. Kilkenny.

Kilkenny, renowned for its Statutes and its castle, for cats and craftsmanship, is a clean limestone town set in a county of mills and healthy farmlands. Pretty Inistioge, loveliest of all Irish villages, is to the south, beyond the Cistercian splendour of Jerpoint Abbey. The first landscape that Bishop Berkeley knew is round about, and on a sunny day in those unexacting hills the goat paths of James Stephens (1882–1950) come to mind.

> The crooked paths
> Go every way
> Upon the hill
> – They wind about
> Through the heather,
> In and out
> Of the quiet
> Sunniness.
> And there the goats,
> Day after day,
> Stray
> In sunny
> Quietness,
> Cropping here,
> And cropping there
> – As they pause,
> And turn
> And pass –
> Now a bit
> Of heather spray,
> Now a mouthful
> Of the grass.

from *The Goat Paths*. James Stephens.

Ireland, Giraldus Cambrensis observed, has no poisonous reptiles. 'It has no serpents or snakes, toads or frogs, tortoises or scorpions. It has no dragons.' But in his time a frog – perhaps indeed the ancestor of all Irish frogs since – was found in Waterford.

> Duvendaldus, the King of Ossory, who happened to be there at the time, with a great shaking of his head and great sorrow in his heart at last said (and he was a man of great wisdom among his people and loyal to them): 'That reptile brings very bad news to Ireland.'

Waterford today looks undismayed, a pleasant watery city, famous for cutting glass. Not far from it the graves of poets mark Ballylaneen and Newtown; and further west, past sing-song Cork, the groves of Blarney are as charming as they were for Richard Alfred Milliken (1767–1815), who was inspired to verse on their behalf. Clonakilty – known once, and sometimes

154

The Blasket Islands, off the coast of Kerry.

even still, as Clonakilty-God-help-us – is brighter than it used to be, gateway to the tourists' West, worthy at last of a more graceful sobriquet. Town of the little boats, colour-washed and narrow, Skibbereen dozes through yet another afternoon. Swift mourned Vanessa at nearby Unionhall, though no one there remarks on that.

Ruins are the memorial stones of the monks of Dingle, and from the Blasket Islands the Brightcity lights have enticed the last of the survivors. But the word of Maurice O'Sullivan (1904–50) remains to remind us of that island life and the idiosyncrasy of its language.

My grandfather and I were lying on the Castle Summit. It was a fine sunny day in July. The sun was splitting the stones with its heat and the grass burnt to the roots. I could see, far away to the south, Iveragh painted in many colours by the sun. South-west were the Skelligs glistening white and the sea around them dotted with fishing-boats from England.

'Isn't it a fine healthy life those fishermen have, daddo?' said I.

I got no answer. Turning round I saw the old man was asleep. I looked at him, thinking. You were one day in the flower of youth, said I in my own mind, but, my sorrow, the skin of your brow is wrinkled now and the hair on your head is grey. You are without suppleness in your limbs and without pleasure in the grand view to be seen from this hill. But, alas, if I live, some day I will be as you are now.

The heat was very great, and so I thought of waking him for fear the sun would kill him. I caught him by his grey beard and gave it a pull.

from *Twenty Years A-Growing.*
Translated from the Irish by Moya Llewelyn Davies and George Thomson.

And Robin Flower, in his foreword to Tomás Ó Crohan's *The Islandman*, supplies the Blasket landscape:

Nearest to the land lies Beginish – a small flat island of good grass. A mile to the west is the Great Blasket – a high, narrow island, three miles by one, with a little cluster of houses on its eastern front towards the mainland, perched on the cliff above the tiny harbour and the long beach of sand called An Tráigh Bhán, the White Strand. Beyond the White Strand to the north there is a cliff-ringed beach of shingle known as the Gravel Strand, on which boats may be pulled up. Here the island sheep are driven for shearing, and on the rocks, out from the beach, weed is gathered for manure. The adventure of the women in Chapter 2 happened here, and here Tomás had his encounter with the seal (Chapter 9). The island rises westward in a series of hills on which the cattle and sheep find scant pasturage and rabbits burrow in the lofty cliffs. The best turf in the island is on its summit, on the hill called Sliabh an Dúna, beyond the prehistoric cliff fort which gives its name to the height, and a rough road leads some way back along the island in that direction. Above the road is an old martello tower, dating from the French wars, which stood unimpaired until a few years ago, when a thunderbolt shattered it. At the end of the island the hill falls away into a grassy expanse, slanting to the south, where was an ancient settlement, of which only fragments of beehive dwellings now remain. Beyond this again the land narrows, and you climb over jagged rocks to Ceann Dubh, Black Head, the extreme western point of the island. A narrow strait separates Ceann Dubh from Inish na Bro, Quern Island, and a little farther off lies Inishvickillaun, where is an ancient church and a little modern house, now only intermittently inhabited. The caves of Ceann Dubh and Inishvickillaun are haunted by seals, and Inish na Bro and Inishvickillaun teem with rabbits. Farther out to the west is the Teeraught, the Western Island, a high pinnacle of rock carrying a lighthouse, the last light that Irish emigrants see on their voyage to America. North of the main island is Inish Tooshkert, the Northern Island, a fastness of cliffs, in which is a well-preserved ancient oratory.

Along the coast, Ralegh and Spenser were entertained at Castlegregory; inland a bit, Seán Ó Tuama held his poet's court at Croom in the 1750s. Kate O'Brien (1897–1974) is Limerick's novelist.

The light of the October day was dropping from afternoon clarity to softness when Anthony Considine led his limping horse round the last curve of the Gap of Storm and halted there to behold the Vale of Honey.
The Vale of Honey is a wide plain of fertile pastures and deep woods, watered by many streams and ringed about by mountains. Westward the Bearnagh hills through whose Gap of Storm the traveller had just tramped, shelter it from the Atlantic-salted wind, and at the foot of these hills a great river sweeps about the western valley, zigzagging passionately westward and southward and westward again in its search for the sea.

A few miles below him on this river's banks the traveller saw the grey blur of a town.

'That must be Mellick', he said to hearten himself and his horse.

In the south two remote green hills had wrapped their heads in cloud; eastward the stonier, bluer peaks wore caps of snow already. To the north the mountains of St Phelim were bronzed and warmly wooded.

Villages lay untidily about the plain; smoke floated from the chimneys of parked mansions and the broken thatch of cowmen's huts; green, blue, brown, in all their shades of dark and brightness, lay folded together across the stretching acres in a colour-tranquillity as absolute as sleep, and which neither the breaking glint of lake and stream nor the seasonal flame of woodtops could disquiet. Lark songs, the thin sibilance of dried leaves, and the crying of milk-heavy cows were all the sounds that came up to the man who stood in the Gap of Storm and scanned the drowsed and age-saddened vista out of eyes that were neither drowsed nor sad.

from *Without My Cloak*.

In this Hardy-esque novel Anthony Considine likens the Vale of Honey to a saucer, the way the little hills come up all round it. But he moves on, in through the crumbling gates of the city, which becomes his own: horse-thief turned respectable by time, businessman and citizen, travelling less dangerously in his prosperity.

Charles Street and his direction along it now went parallel with the seaward flow of the river. At the crossings, where short streets cut the New Town symmetrically from east to west, he could glimpse the great stream to the right of him down a short hill and observe the regular hurry of its course past the unhurrying docks; carts and ships and cargoes he noted, his own and other men's, and all he saw refreshed his knowledge of the town's business life and kept the surface of his mind in motion with trade affairs. When he looked eastward up the wide crossing streets, he snatched, one block away, a fragment of the life of King's Street, where the shops were gay at this hour, and where broughams and phaëtons splashed arrogantly through the mud, bearing wives and daughters of the town to and fro between the tall brown houses at the southern end and all the fripperies and agitations of their social habit. The street in which they rode was a lively place compared with its long grey parallel where Anthony was walking. Charles Street consisted mainly of stores and offices; it wore the grave, grey look of commerce, an aspect increased by the dusty pallor laid on the street's face by two or three great flour mills. Drays and carts were its chief traffic, interspersed by the occasional phaëtons of the merchants.

The Shannon widens at Limerick and becomes the sea. It is the river that 'rightly holds the chief place among all the rivers of Ireland whether old or new, both on account of the magnificence of its size, its long meanderings, and its abundance of fish'. Giraldus was very fond of fish. 'This country, above all others we have seen, is well supplied with beautiful lakes, full of fish and very large.' The sea-coasts 'abound with sea-fish', the Shannon 'with lampreys'.

Silent men with pipes entice this wealth from the waters in these tourist times, Irishmen and French, German, English, American, Scandinavian – and of as many nationalities are the botanists who become excited on the flat stone slabs of the Burren, which hasn't changed a bit in all its years. Rain has washed the goodness into fissured niches, laying out a desert for modest blooms to cheer. The very bones of Ireland's landscape break through its skin on the Burren, as they do on the mountains of Connacht and Donegal. The wild flowers seem like a compensation in so much harshness, as does the magic picture which Roderic O'Flaherty recorded in the seventeenth century of:

that inchanted island called O'Brasil, and in Irish Beg-ara or the Lesser Aran, set down in cards of navigation. Whether it be reall and firm land, kept hidden by special ordinance of God, as the terrestiall paradise, or else some illusion of airy clouds appearing on the surface of the sea, or the craft of evil spirits, is more than our judgements can sound out. There is, westward of Aran, in sight of the next continent of Balynahynsy barony, Skerde, a wild island of huge rocks, the receptacle of a deale of seales thereon yearly slaughtered. These rocks sometimes appear to be a great city far of, full of houses, castles, towers, and chimneys; sometimes full of blazing flames, smoak, and people running to and fro. Another day you would see nothing but a number of ships, with their sailes and riggings; then so many great stakes or reekes of corn and turf; and this not only on fair sun-shining dayes, whereby it might be thought the reflection of the sun-beamse, on the vapours arising about it, had been the cause, but alsoe on dark and cloudy days happening. There is another like number of rocks, called Carrigmeacan, on the same coast, whereon the like apparitions are seen. But the inchanted island of O'Brasil is not always visible, as those rocks are, nor these rocks have allways those apparitions.

from *West or H-Iar Connaught*.

Tinkers' washing dangles from wayside barbed wire of the West, but those are happy tourists who jog along in gaily painted caravans, hired to them by the fortnight: the tinkers occupy the streamlined ones. Higgledy-piggledy the travelling people are scattered all over untidy Ireland, another aspect of its landscape as travelling people have always been. All around them there's more litter than in the past, more plastic bags that rain cannot destroy.

City of the Tribes yet without tribes now, Galway manages well enough: washed to a quiet greyness, ancient and modern stone unites as best it can. 'A town tormented by the sea', a forgotten poet considered, and the place's story-teller is remembered rather better: the gentle Pádraic Ó Conaire twinkles like a garden gnome in front of the Bank of Ireland and is honoured on the dinner menu of the Great Southern Hotel – *Turbot Ó Conaire* or something similar.

Some say Ross House, the barracks where Violet Martin lived, is up for sale, others contradict the rumour. But at least there can be no doubt that it is less

Estuary of the River Shannon, below Limerick.

beautiful than Lough Corrib, which it surveys. Renvyle was the home of
Oliver St John Gogarty, Moycullen the birthplace of Roderic O'Flaherty.

> On the north-west of Balynahinsy, are the twelve high mountains of Bennabeola,
> called by marriners the twelve stakes, being the first land they discover as they come
> from the maine. Bindon glass is the highest of them, and, next the lake, is two miles
> high and hath standing water on the top of it, wherein they say if any washeth his
> head, he becomes hoare.
>
> <div align="right">from <i>West or H-Iar Connaught.</i></div>

They're known as the Twelve Pins now, towering over the brown-black
bogs of Connemara, where sleek Volvos and Austins draw in the turf and there
isn't a red petticoat in sight. In air-conditioned buses the tourists amble through
Ireland's most arresting landscape, glimpsing the Devil's Mother and Ben-
gorm, nodding off in Letterfrack. Máirtín Ó Cadhain was of these parts, of 'a
race whose guardian angel was the American trunk, whose guiding star was the
exile ship, whose Red Sea was the Atlantic'. One of his timid Galway girls,
preparing for her emigration to America, would take with her the very
mountains, the streams and stone walls she had known all her life. She makes do
with a sod of turf and a chip hacked off the hearthstone, a posy of withered
shamrock.

The strands of Achill Island, where Richard Brinsley Sheridan had poor relations, are dotted with the summer visitors Mary Lavin wrote of. Inland again, lines have been composed to sweeten Mulrany; Lough Feeagh may yet be an inspiration for someone. Cursed for its murders, a hillside near Ballycroy seems innocent in the afternoon sun; a bohreen dance-hall is silent as the grave. 'I knew the Playboy of the Western World,' an old man says. 'And the Red Pedlar too, who murdered on that hill.' Stories thrive, no matter what the land is like.

Collooney has a ballad about its priest; Enniskillen schooled Wilde and Beckett. Donegal's Lough Derg is still a place of pilgrimage, faith for ever keeping faith.

> From Cavan and from Leitrim and from Mayo,
> From all the thin-faced parishes where hills
> Are perished noses running peaty water,
> They come to Lough Derg to fast and pray and beg . . .
>   from *Lough Derg*. Patrick Kavanagh (1905–67).

All Ireland meets at Kavanagh's rendezvous: the baker from Rathfriland, the solicitor from Derry, the Castleblayney grocer, Wicklow priest and Kerry civil servant, 'wives whose husbands have taken to drinking'.

> But there were the sincere as well
> The innocent who feared the hell
> Of sin. The girl who had won
> A lover and the girl who had none
> Were both in trouble
> Trying to encave in the rubble
> Of these rocks the Real,
> The part that can feel.
> And the half-pilgrims too,
> They who are the true
> Spirit of Ireland, who joke
> Through the Death-mask and take
> Virgins of heaven or flesh,
> Were on Lough Derg Island
> Wanting some half-wish.

> Over the black waves of the lake trip the last echoes
> Of the bell that has shooed through the chapel door
> The last pilgrims, like hens to roost,
> The sun through Fermanagh's furze fingers
> Looks now on the deserted penance rings of stone
> Where only John Flood on St Kevin's Bed lingers
> With the sexton's heaven-sure stance, the man who knows

The ins and outs of religion . . .
'Hail glorious St Patrick' a girl sings above
The old-man drone of the harmonium.
The rosary is said and Benediction.
The sacramental sun turns round and 'Holy, Holy, Holy'
The pilgrims cry, striking their breasts in Purgatory.
The same routine and ritual now
As serves for street processions or congresses
That take all shapes of souls as a living theme
In a novel refuses nothing. No truth oppresses.

from *Lough Derg*.

Sean O'Faolain brings the pilgrimage proceedings even more up to date:

Beyond the four or five whitewashed houses – she guessed that they had been the only buildings before trains and buses made the pilgrimage popular – and beyond the cement paths, she came on the remains of the natural island: a knoll, some warm grass, the tree, and the roots of the old hermit's cells across whose teeth of stone barefooted pilgrims were already treading on one another's heels. Most of these barefooted people wore mackintoshes. They not only stumbled on one another's heels, they kneeled on one another's toes and tails; for the island was crowded – she thought there must be nearly two thousand people on it.

from *Lovers of the Lake*.

Ballad-makers wandered these ways in Donegal and Mayo and Fermanagh. Beggar people and tinkers marked in their minds the trees and houses. Padraic Colum's drover made the weary trek from the 'wet hills by the sea' through Leitrim and Longford to 'Meath of the pastures', one man alone with his cattle.

I hear in the darkness
Their slipping and breathing –
I name them the by-ways
They're to pass without heeding;

Then the wet, winding roads,
Brown bogs with black water,
And my thoughts on white ships
And the King o' Spain's daughter.

from *A Drover*.

In Derry, battle-scarred and bitter, you think of St Columba, the lonely Colmcille, dove of the Church. Derry could do with his prayers today, could do with being reminded that once it was his precious place, his beloved little grove.

Plentiful in the West the fruit of the apple-tree,
Many kings and princes;

161

Plentiful are luxurious sloes,
Plentiful oak-woods of noble mast.

Melodious her clerics, melodious her birds,
Gentle her youths, wise her elders,
Illustrious her men, famous to behold,
Illustrious her women for fond espousal.

.   .   .

Were all Alba mine
From its centre to its border,
I would rather have the site of a house
In the middle of fair Derry.

from *Colum Cille's Greeting to Ireland.*
Translated from the Irish by Kuno Meyer.

Give Derry back to Colmcille, you plead, surveying the aftermath of violence and destruction. You turn away, seeking consolation in his devotion to this place, and in his uncomplicated history. He was descended on his father's side from Niall of the Nine Hostages, high king of Ireland, and from Leinster royalty on his mother's. On Lough Foyle, at Moville, he was prepared for the religious life; in 546 he founded his church in Derry itself. He travelled widely throughout Ireland, preaching and converting, founding monasteries at Durrow and Kells. The story is told that while he was on a return visit to the monastery at Moville his love of books caused him to copy, surreptitiously, the monastery's edition of St Jerome's psalter, which had been obtained with great difficulty in Rome. Trouble ensued when this liberty was discovered, the abbot claiming that any copy made must belong to him, Columba vigorously disagreeing. 'To every cow her calf,' was the judgment of the High King, to whom the case was eventually taken, 'and to every book its copy.' Columba refused to accept this verdict, and the dispute led to war between his royal kinsmen of Ulster and the High King. It was in penance, because of that slaughter caused by himself, that he went into exile on Iona, determined to convert as many pagan souls in Scotland and the north of England as there had been victims in the conflict. He was Ireland's first notable exile: not far from Derry, over the Donegal border, there was a farewell as sorrowful as the withered shamrock packed into a trunk or William Allingham's adieu to Ballyshannon. Benedict Kiely evokes that sombre mood:

In Colmcille's Glen of Gartan, near Letterkenny, you can still see the Flagstone of Loneliness, Leac an Uaignis, on which, tradition held, the saint had slept penitentially on the night before he sailed from Ireland. Right into our time men and women going into exile would make the *turas*, or pilgrimage, to and around the Glen of Gartan, and lie on that stone and pray to the saint, who was also a poet, to be preserved against the pangs of homesickness.

162

Derry. Celebrations for St Columba's Day, 15 June, in the relative peace of the early 1960s.

My Derry, my little oak-grove,
My dwelling and my little cell,
O living God that art in Heaven above,
Woe to him who violates it!
(*Colum Cille's Greeting to Ireland.* Translated from the Irish by Kuno Meyer)

From the heart of his loneliness the poet-saint afterwards woefully remembered the seagulls of Lough Foyle, the towns of Durrow and Derry, and Ireland's ragged coast, which he loved with a passion that made him weep.

> On some island I long to be,
> a rocky promontory, looking on
> the coiling surface of the sea.
>
> To see the waves, crest on crest
> of the great shining ocean, composing
> a hymn to the creator, without rest.
>
> To see without sadness the strand
> lined with bright shells, and birds
> lamenting overhead, a lonely sound.
>
> To hear the whisper of small waves
> against the rocks, that endless sea-
> sound, like keening over graves.
>
> To watch the sea-birds sailing
> in flocks, and most marvellous
> of monsters, the turning whale.
>
> To see the shift from ebbtide
> to flood and tell my secret name:
> 'He who set his back on Ireland.'
>
> Translated from the Irish by John Montague.

The Halls, in the 1830s and '40s, particularly enjoyed Ulster. No wonder: it is a likable province. There is a rural tidiness, a well-kept look. Margaret Barrington (1896–1982) in her remarkable short stories wraps husbandry and landscape together, the blue Sperrin mountains shimmering distantly in a haze, the smell of retting flax heavy on the air, hard and honest farming throwing up images of its own.

> Every evening when dusk was falling, he would stand at the front door of his great farmhouse and gaze across the fields, reckoning the yield of this field or that, wondering what price the crops would fetch, looking at his great flax-pits, the largest in all the lands that border on Lough Neagh. Then filled with pride, he would watch his cows being driven from the pastures for the milking and count them as they came, one by one, their heads bent, their udders heavy with milk. Then he would follow them to the byre and watch his daughter Tamar milk, her lovely, young, red head resting against the cow's silken flank, and listen to her young voice as she sang some country song while the milk flowed in long regular squirts into the great can between her legs.
>
> from *David's Daughter, Tamar.*

Ulster's wilder landscape: Ballintoy, Co. Antrim.

But not all of Ulster is tame Tyrone or pretty Fermanagh. Its wilder landscape, especially that of Antrim, is as spectacular as any in Ireland. It is bounded, the Halls dutifully noted, 'on the north by the Northern Ocean, on the east and north-east by the North Channel, on the south-east by Belfast Lough and the river Lagan, which separate it from the county of Down; on the south by the county of Down; on the south-west by Lough Neagh, and on the west by the county of Londonderry – the river Bann, which issues from Lough Beg, dividing the two counties, but leaving the Liberties of Coleraine, as the north-west boundary of Antrim. It is therefore encompassed by water – on the west and south-west by the magnificent river Bann, and the great inland sea, Lough Neagh; on the south and south-east by the river Lagan and Belfast Lough; and on all other sides by the ocean. Hence its ancient name, Endruim, "the habitation upon the waters" – easily corrupted into Antrim.'

Lough Neagh, Ulster's single eye, is another of Giraldus's wonders, full to the brim with fish:

There is a lake in Ulster of a remarkable size. It is thirty miles long and fifteen miles wide. From it a very beautiful river called the Bann flows into the northern ocean. Here the fishermen complain not of a scarcity of fish, but of too great catches and the breaking of their nets. In our time a fish was caught here one that had come down from the lake, and not from the sea – which had the shape more or less of a salmon, and was of such size that it could not be dragged or carried as a whole. Accordingly it was cut up and carried about through the province.

They say that an accident was responsible for the rise of this remarkable lake. There was from ancient times in the region now covered by the lake a people very much given to vice, and particularly addicted, above any other people in Ireland, to bestiality. There was a saying well known to that people that if a certain well of the district which, because of a great fear of it that had been inherited from a barbarous superstition, was always covered and sealed, should be left uncovered, it would immediately overflow to such an extent that it would wipe out and destroy the whole district and people. It happened, however, that a young woman came to the well to draw water. She filled her vessel, and, before covering the well, ran quickly to her little child, because she had heard him crying where she had placed him a little way off. But 'the voice of the people is the voice of God', and when she hurried back she met such an overflow from the well that both herself and her boy were swept off immediately. Within an hour the whole people and their flocks were overwhelmed in this local and provincial flood. The whole area was covered with a sea of water which remained there and made a permanent lake.

It looked as if the author of nature had judged that a land which had known such filthy crimes against nature was unworthy not only of its first inhabitants but of any others in the future.

There is some confirmation of this story in as much as fishermen of the lake clearly see under the waves in calm weather towers of churches, which, as is usual in that country, are tall, slender, and rounded.

Co. Down the Halls found remarkable for 'its inequality of surface; for, although the mountains are chiefly confined to the southern district, where they are magnificent, the lesser hills are abundant in all parts; hence it is said to have derived its ancient name, Dunum, "which signifies a hill, or a hilly country." This peculiar character – a perpetual rise and fall in the landscape – renders it highly picturesque; it is not ill wooded; it contains many rivers; the ocean is its boundary on three sides; and the huge inland sea, "Strangford Lough," forms another striking and interesting feature of the county.'

The Halls run out of steam somewhat in Belfast, satisfying themselves with references to its 'commercial character', its botanical gardens, charitable institutions and banking facilities. 'The high tone which literature and science have given to its people, have, as it were, created a somewhat peculiar class; for knowledge elevates while it improves; and a large proportion of the merchants and manufacturers of Belfast are "gentry" in the most emphatic sense of the term; education, and a thirst for learning, having, in a remarkable degree, prevented the sordid habits too frequently engendered by trade.' The Halls joyfully avow that the British temperance movement was born in Belfast, due to 'terrible necessity'. The neighbouring landscape, they add, is picturesque.

The eerie and compelling landscape of the Burren, Co. Clare.

Belfast has been hammered out between Down and Antrim, built to last by enterprise and integrity and commercial good sense. Once a wealth of ships and linen, it's a city that's pawky still with pride. Beneath the grey Antrim mountains, its granite spirit cannot be broken, its face is re-set every day in resolution. 'Devout, profane and hard', Louis MacNeice (1907–63) designated his native city.

> Built on reclaimed mud, hammers playing in the shipyard,
> Time punched with holes like a steel sheet, time
> Hardening the faces, veneering with a grey and speckled rime
> The faces under the shawls and cape:
> This was my mother-city, these my paps.
>
> from *Valediction*.

Yet when the sun shines on this city, and when its people smile, there is a warmth that does you good to be close to. They drive a bargain in Belfast but give you a cup of tea and fresh-baked farls to go with it. And out beyond those hard grey streets, landscaped now with foreign soldiers, war can sometimes be forgotten. Self-important helicopters do not for ever bluster beneath the clouds, barricades come somewhere to an end. Over Belfast Lough the birds still sing, as disdainful of human folly as birds have always been.

> The whistle
> of the bright
> yellow billed
>   little bird:
> Over the loch
> upon a golden
> whin, a blackbird
>   stirred.
>
> *Belfast Lough*. Anonymous.
> Translated from the Irish by John Montague.

Forrest Reid (1875–1947) was Belfast's novelist but his most memorable landscape belongs outside that city, in country gardens, in meadows and on sunny banks. A private writer, free of histrionics and frills, Reid's evocations of childhood's jungle are limpid pictures, faded at the edges, like photographs forgotten in a drawer.

The July sun was warm and sleepy; bees swung in the tall foxgloves; and down below, the slow, long, listless splash of the sea on the white beach sounded dreamily.

The cleanly and bustling appearance of Belfast is decidedly un-national. That it is in Ireland, but not of it, is a remark ever on the lips of visitors from the south or west. (Ireland: Its Scenery, Character, etc.: Mr and Mrs S. C. Hall)

A haunted sea! – blue, deep blue, with a narrow line of white foam where the waves curled over on the pale, glittering sand . . .

from *A Garden by the Sea*.

He kept to the meadow side, and on the opposite bank the leaning trees made little magic caves tapestried with green. Black flies darted restlessly about, and every now and again he heard strange splashes – splashes of birds, of fish; the splash of a rat; and once the heavy, floundering splash of the cow herself, plunging into the water up to her knees . . .

from *Courage*.

The six British counties of Ulster vary in the attention they have received from the men of violence in the present troubles. Political graffiti, once simple in their proclamation of faith kept with monarchy or Pope, are uglier now and point the way to where the war is. The letters of incitement spell murder, intolerance and cruelty. Graffiti, even before they have appeared, haunt the urban landscape, their ugliness resounding as Ulster people go about their lives. Louis MacNeice's poem, *Prospect*, aptly belongs to this unsettled North that once was Ireland's pride:

> Though loves languish and sour
> Fruit puts the teeth on edge,
> Though the ragged nests are empty of song
> In the barbed and blistered hedge,
>
> Though old men's lives and children's bricks
> Spell out a Machiavellian creed,
> Though the evil Past is ever present
> And the happy Present is past indeed,
>
> Though the stone grows and grows
> That we roll up the hill
> And the hill grows and grows
> And gravity conquers still,
>
> Though Nature's laws exploit
> And defeat anarchic men,
> Though every sandcastle concept
> Being *ad hoc* must crumble again,
>
> And though to-day is arid,
> We know – and knowing bless –
> That rooted in futurity
> There is a plant of tenderness.

The poet W. R. Rodgers (1909–69) was also born in Belfast, though he is perhaps more closely associated with Armagh, where he was a Presbyterian minister for many years. Ireland for him was Ulster.

Lower Falls area, West Belfast. Heavily bombed in the last war, the city has – before and since – had more than its share of battering. Edmund Spenser lists it among the 'good towns and strong-holds' destroyed in 1315 by Edward Bruce. According to Mr and Mrs S. C. Hall, in their 19th-century guidebook, its castle was reduced to ruins in both 1503 and 1512 by the Lord Deputy Kildare.

> O these lakes and all gills that live in them,
> These acres and all legs that walk on them,
> These tall winds and all wings that cling to them,
> Are part and parcel of me, bit and bundle,
> Thumb and thimble. Them I am, but none more
> Than the mountains of Mourne that turn and trundle
> Roundly like slow coils of oil along the shore
> of Down and on inland . . .

from *Ireland.*

The Irish, colonizing Scotland long ago, developed then their own colonial *persona*, which was returned with interest to Ulster in the early seventeenth century. That double colonialism, allied to a straightforward way of looking at things and a pioneering drive, keeps Ulster trim. Well-slated tidy houses, domestic farmlands, matter-of-fact fences, combine to impose a gauzy surface on Rodgers' vision of timeless Ireland.

                            There in the hard light
Dark birds, pink-footed, dab and pick
Among the addery roots and marrowy stones,
And the blown waves blink and hiccup at the lake's
Lip. A late bee blares and drones on inland
Into a cone-point of silence, and I
Lying at the rhododendron's foot
Look through five fingers' grille at the lake
Shaking, at the bare and backward plain, and
The running and bending hills that carry
Like a conveyor belt the bright snail-line
Of clouds along the sky all day unendingly.

There, far from the slack noose of rumour
That tightens into choking fact, I relax,
And sound and sights and scents sail slowly by.
But suddenly, like delicate and tilted italics,
The up-standing birds stretch urgently away
Into the sky as suddenly grown grey.
Night rounds on Europe now. And I must go.
Before its hostile faces peer and pour
Over the mind's rim enveloping me,
And my so-frightened thoughts dart here and there
Like trout among their grim stony gazes.

                                        An Irish Lake.

For John Hewitt (b. 1907), another Belfast poet, Ulster is Ireland too:

Groined by deep glens and walled along the west
by the bare hilltops and the tufted moors,
this rim of arable that ends in foam
has but to drop a leaf or snap a branch
and my hand twitches with the leaping verse
as hazel twig will wrench the straining wrists
for untapped jet that thrusts beneath the sod.

Not these my people, of a vainer faith
and a more violent lineage. My dead
lie in the steepled hillock of Kilmore
in a fat country rich with bloom and fruit.
My days, the busy days I owe the world,
are bound to paved unerring roads and rooms
heavy with talk of politics and art.
I cannot spare more than a common phrase
of crops and weather when I pace these lanes

and pause at hedge gap spying on their skill,
so many fences stretch between our minds.

I fear their creed as we have always feared
the lifted hand between the mind and truth.
I know their savage history of wrong
and would at moments lend an eager voice,
if voice avail, to set that tally straight.

And yet no other corner in this land
offers in shape and colour all I need
for sight to torch the mind with living light.

The Glens.

Patrick Kavanagh belonged to Ulster's border country, to the limbo-lands of Monaghan, next door to W. R. Rodgers' Armagh.

My black hills have never seen the sun rising,
Eternally they look north towards Armagh.
Lot's wife would not be salt if she had been
Incurious as my black hills that are happy
When dawn whitens Glassdrummond chapel.

My hills hoard the bright shillings of March
While the sun searches in every pocket.
They are my Alps and I have climbed the Matterhorn
With a sheaf of hay for three perishing calves
In the field under the Big Forth of Rocksavage.

The sleety winds fondle the rushy beards of Shancoduff
While the cattle-drovers sheltering in the Featherna Bush
Look up and say: 'Who owns them hungry hills
That the water-hen and snipe must have forsaken?
A poet? Then by heavens he must be poor.'
I hear and is my heart not badly shaken?

Shancoduff.

Through Ballybay and Carrickmacross, south to Slane, east along the valley of the Boyne. One fateful field is pointed out: where Orange William slept the night before his most auspicious battle. At Monasterboice the finest of Ireland's High Crosses carelessly survive the weathers and the years; by the River Mattock the Cistercians' honey fountain   Mellifont Abbey – nestles in untroubled peace. At Knowth and Dowth and New Grange the burial metropolis that changed the landscape stubbornly keeps its secrets.

Brash roadside lounge-bars, concrete convents, unpretty bungalows; good farming land, good business towns, crowded Navan, historic Trim. The elder-tree castle which once housed King John needs no protection from Brightcity culture; little Bective, Mellifont's daughter, long ago lost her church.

Looking across Co. Meath from Tara, 'the Hill of Kings'.

From the heights of Tara the great plain of Meath stretches for ever: high kings' panorama, a royal view of Ireland's least impressive landscape. Yet sentiment insists that Ireland is encapsuled here: history, geography, landscape, its literature, its living and its dead. Tara, like the Boyne Valley graveyards, goes back beyond imagination, an older sanctity honoured by Celtic generations. Grass has taken over, but when you stand where there was once a palace, gazing out across those massive plains, you think of Rath Cruachan lost also in the west and Emain Macha in the north. Cúchulainn's country is nearer, Swift's Laracor almost within sight. Those long fat pastures immediately below are the native landscape of the poet Francis Ledwidge (1891–1917).

> The hedges are all drowned in green grass seas,
> And bobbing poppies flare like Elmo's light,
> While siren-like the pollen-stainéd bees
> Drone in the clover depths. And up the height
> The cuckoo's voice is hoarse and broke with joy.
> And on the lowland crops the crows make raid,
> Nor fear the clappers of the farmer's boy,
> Who sleeps, like drunken Noah, in the shade.

from *June*.

174

From the breezy vantage heights of Tara, Ireland then and now is spread around. Ireland's places and all the words that have recorded them, all the art that has reflected them, all the affection that has touched them: in a riot of confusion the mind fills up. And then a valediction challenges the flapping wind and calmly offers a final Irish message.

If I were a dog of sunlight I would bound
From Phoenix Park to Achill Sound,
Picking up the scent of a hundred fugitives
That have broken the mesh of ordinary lives,
But being ordinary too I must in course discuss
What we mean to Ireland or Ireland to us;
I have to observe milestone and curio
The beaten buried gold of an old king's bravado,
Falsetto antiquities, I have to gesture,
Take part in, or renounce, each imposture;
Therefore I resign, good-bye the chequered and the quiet hills
The gaudily-striped Atlantic, the linen-mills
That swallow the shawled file, the black moor where half
A turf-stack stands like a ruined cenotaph;
Good-bye your hens running in and out of the white house
Your absent-minded goats along the road, your black cows
Your greyhounds and your hunters beautifully bred
Your drums and your dolled-up Virgins and your ignorant dead.

from Valediction. Louis MacNeice.

For Louis MacNeice, two powerful images of Ireland: the 'dolled-up Virgins' and the cenotaph-like turf stack.

Postscript

Many of the English versions of Irish poems in this book have been by contemporary Irish writers who are distinguished poets in their own right – John Montague, Seamus Heaney, Eavan Boland, Thomas Kinsella, Brendan Kennelly and others. With a continuing relevance to landscape, there has also been some original work by a very small handful of Ireland's senior living practitioners. Any further contribution from the present belongs to a final chapter that only time can dictate. Landscape changes, or does not. Writing becomes literature, or does not. Time alone lays down the law.

But two voices among those of the many poets and fiction-writers of today may perhaps speak for all of them. Derek Mahon adds another farewell to MacNeice's own:

> Your ashes will not stir, even on this high ground,
> However the wind tugs, the headstones shake –
> This plot is consecrated, for your sake,
> To what lies in the future tense. You lie
> Past tension now, and spring is coming round
> Igniting flowers on the peninsula.
>
> from *In Carrowdore Churchyard*

And Michael Longley turns the wheel full circle almost, swivelling us back to the heyday of the Irish Celts, to the Aran they made their own:

> Summer and solstice as the seasons turn
> Anchor our boat in a perfect standstill,
> The harbour wall of Inishmore astern
> Where the Atlantic waters overspill –
> I shall name this the point of no return . . .
>
> from *Leaving Inishmore*

Aran Islands, 'Where the Atlantic waters overspill', photographed by J. M. Synge.

Bibliography

Margaret Barrington, *David's Daughter, Tamar and Other Stories*, Dublin 1982

Elizabeth Bowen, *Collected Stories*, London 1980

Giraldus Cambrensis, *The History and Topography of Ireland*, translated by John J. O'Meara, London 1951

Maurice Collis, *Somerville and Ross*, London 1968

Padraic Colum, *Poems*, New York 1932

Daniel Corkery, *The Hidden Ireland*, Dublin 1925

———, *The Wager and Other Stories*, New York 1950

———, *Synge and Anglo-Irish Literature*, Cork 1931

Barry Cunliffe, *The Celtic World*, London 1979

Edmund Curtis, *A History of Ireland*, London 1936

Brian de Breffny (ed.), *The Irish World*, London 1977

Terence de Vere White, *The Anglo-Irish*, London 1972

Eilis Dillon, *Inside Ireland*, London 1982

Richard Ellmann, *Letters of James Joyce*, London 1966

Lady Gregory, *Journals 1916–1930*, London 1946

Mrs and Mrs S. C. Hall, *A Week in Killarney*, London 1850

———, *Ireland: Its Scenery, Character, etc.*, 3 vols., London 1841, 1842, 1843

Kieran Hickey, *The Light of Other Days*, London 1973

Kenneth Hurlstone Jackson, *A Celtic Miscellany*, London 1951

Nevill Johnson, *Dublin: The People's City*, Dublin 1981

Brendan Kennelly (ed.), *The Penguin Book of Irish Verse*, London 1970

Benedict Kiely (ed.), *The Penguin Book of Irish Short Stories*, London 1981

———, *Poor Scholar: A Study of Wm Carleton*, Dublin 1947

Thomas Kinsella (trans.) *The Táin*, London 1969

Mary Lavin, *Happiness and Other Stories*, London 1969

W. R. Le Fanu, *Seventy Years of Irish Life*, London 1893

Seumas MacManus (ed.), *Donegal Fairy Stories*, London 1902

Seán Mac Réamoinn (ed.), *Gaelic Poetry*, London 1982

Edward Malins and Patrick Bowe, *Irish Gardens and Demesnes since 1830*, London 1980

Edward Malins and The Knight of Glin, *Lost Demesnes; Irish Landscape Gardening 1660–1845*, London 1976

David Marcus (ed.), *The Bodley Head Book of Irish Short Stories*, London 1980

J. Markale, *Les Celtes et la Civilisation Celtique*, Paris 1976

Michael McLaverty, *Collected Stories*, Dublin 1978

Brian Merriman, *The Midnight Court*, translated by David Marcus, Dublin 1953

Kuno Meyer, *Ancient Irish Poetry*, London 1913

John Montague (ed.), *Faber Book of Irish Verse*, London 1974

178

George Moore, *The Untilled Field*, London 1976

Eoin Neeson, *The Book of Irish Saints*, Cork 1967

Flann O'Brien, *At Swim-Two-Birds*, London 1939

Kate O'Brien, *Without My Cloak*, London 1949

Maírtín Ó Cadhain, *The Road to Brightcity*, Dublin 1981

Sean O'Casey, *I Knock at the Door*, London 1939

Frank O'Connor, *A Book of Ireland*, London 1959

———, *Collected Stories*, New York, 1981

Tomás Ó Crohan, *The Islandman*, foreword by Robin Flower, Oxford 1951

Sean O'Faolain, *The Irish*, London 1947

———, *Collected Stories*, New York, 1981

Liam O'Flaherty, *The Pedlar's Revenge*, Dublin 1976

Roderic O'Flaherty, *West or H-Iar Connaught*, Dublin 1846

Seumas O'Kelly, *The Weaver's Grave*, Dublin 1965

Maurice O'Sullivan, *Twenty Years A-Growing*, London 1953

Seán Ó Tuama, *Without My Cloak*, London 1949

James Plunkett, *The Gems She Wore*, London 1972

Forrest Reid, *A Garden by the Sea and Other Stories*, London 1918

Edith Somerville and Martin Ross, *Through Connemara in a Governess Cart*, London 1893

———, *Experiences of an Irish R. M.*, London 1944

Peter Somerville-Large, *The Grand Irish Tour*, London 1982

James Stephens, *Collected Poems*, London 1965

J. M. Synge, *Collected Works*, London 1966

William Thackeray, *Irish Sketch-Book*, 2 vols., London 1843

David Thomson and Moyra McGusty (ed.), *The Irish Journals of Elizabeth Smith 1840–1850*, London 1980

Cecil Woodham Smith, *The Great Hunger*, London 1962

Arthur Young, *A Tour of Ireland 1776–1779*, London 1780

Sources of Quotations

Pp. 32, 33, Seamus Heaney quoted from Séan Mac Réamoinn: *Gaelic Poetry*; p. 56, Edward Malins and The Knight of Glin quoted from *Lost Demesnes*; p. 59, The Reverend Delany's poem quoted from Edward Malins: *Lost Demesnes*; p. 65, Edward Willes quoted from Edward Malins: *Lost Demesnes*; p. 92, Seamus Heaney quoted from Séan Mac Réamoinn: *Gaelic Poetry*; p. 109, Lady Gregory quoted from her *Journals 1916–1930*; p. 111, Violet Martin quoted from Maurice Collis: *Somerville and Ross*; p. 130, James Joyce quoted from Richard Ellmann: *Letters of James Joyce*; pp. 130, 131, Sean O'Casey quoted from his autobiography, *I Knock at the Door*; pp. 143, 144, David Marcus quoted from his introduction to *The Bodley Head Book of Irish Short Stories*; p. 162, Benedict Kiely quoted from Séan Mac Réamoinn: *Gaelic Poetry*.

Acknowledgments

Permission to use copyright material is gratefully acknowledged to the following:

John Betjeman and John Murray (Publishers) Ltd for permission to reprint 'Ireland with Emily' from *Collected Poems* by John Betjeman; Austin Clarke and The Dolmen Press for permission to reprint 'Beyond the Pale' from *Flight to Africa* by Austin Clarke; Lucy Rodgers Cohen for permission to reprint 'An Irish Lake', © The Estate of W. R. Rodgers 1941; Faber and Faber Ltd for permission to reprint 'The Bushy, Leafy Oaktree' (translation) from *Sweeney* by Seamus Heaney, and for permission to reprint 'Prospect' and an extract from 'Valediction' from the *Collected Poems of Louis MacNeice*; Farrar, Straus & Giroux for permission to reprint 'The Bushy, Leafy Oaktree' from *Sweeney Astray* © 1977, 1984 by Seamus Heaney; Granada Publishing Ltd and the estate of the late Flann O'Brien (translator) for permission to reprint 'A Hedge Before Me'; John Hewitt for permission to reprint 'The Glens' from *The Selected John Hewitt*, edited with an introduction by Alan Warner (Blackstaff Press, 1981); Katherine B. Kavanagh for permission to reprint 'Shancoduff' and an extract from 'Lough Derg' by Patrick Kavanagh; Brendan Kennelly (translator) and Penguin Books Ltd for permission to reprint 'The Old Woman of Beare' and 'My Story' from *The Penguin Book of Irish Verse*; Thomas Kinsella (translator) and The Dolmen Press for permission to reprint extracts from *The Táin*; Sean O'Faolain (translator) and Penguin Books Ltd for permission to reprint 'The Flight of Diarmuid and Grainne' from *The Irish,* © Sean O'Faolain 1969, 1980; John J. O'Meara (translator) and The Dolmen Press for permission to reprint extracts from Giraldus Cambrensis, *The History and Topography of Ireland*; Oxford University Press for permission to reprint from Robin Flower's foreword to his translation of *The Islandman* by T. Ó Crohan (1951); A. D. Peters and Co Ltd and Joan Daves (US) for permission to reprint 'The Hermit's Song', 'Storm at Sea', 'The Tipperary Woodlands' and extracts from 'The Sweetness of Nature', 'The Lament for Art O'Leary', 'Kilcash', © 1959 by Frank O'Connor, (translator); A. D. Peters and Co Ltd for permission to reprint 'On Some Island I Long to Be' and 'The Whistle' by John Montague (translator); Michael B. Yeats, Anne Yeats and Macmillan, London, Limited for permission to reprint extracts from the poetry of W. B. Yeats taken from *The Collected Poems* by W. B. Yeats; and to Macmillan Publishing Company for permission to reprint selections from *Collected Poems* by W. B. Yeats and for permission to reprint an extract from 'In Memory of Eva Gore-Booth and Con Markiewicz' from *Collected Poems* by W. B. Yeats, © 1928 by Macmillan Publishing Company, Inc., renewed 1956 by Georgie Yeats.

Index

Numbers in italics refer to illustrations and their captions

Sources of Illustrations

Black and white illustrations

BELFAST Historic Monuments Branch p. 13; Northern Ireland Tourist Board p. 27; Ulster Museum p. 57: BELZEAUX pp. 9, 43, 49: CAMBRIDGE UNIVERSITY Director in Aerial Photography p. 15: P. CHEZE-BROWN p. 50: DUBLIN Commissioners of Public Works p. 42; Bord Fáilte pp. 10, 23, 29, 52, 114, 116, 123, 175 (right); National Gallery of Ireland pp. 59, 111; National Library of Ireland pp. 73, 128, 131; Trinity College Library pp. 121, 122, 177: Courtesy MISS GORE-BOOTH p. 115: RICHARD HAUGHTON pp. 2–3, 53, 55, 69, 97, 103, 105, 107, 129, 133, 135, 139, 143, 144, 147, 155, 175 (left): LONDON Victoria and Albert Museum p. 66: G. MOTT p. 85: OXFORD Bodleian Library p. 106: Courtesy RANK ORGANIZATION p. 141: EDWIN SMITH pp. 41, 45, 81, 83, 93, 113, 119, 125, 153, 163, 165, 174: C. SMYTHE p. 109: SOURCE LIBRARY pp. 25, 47, 117, 159: C. STEELE-PERKINS p. 171: THAMES AND HUDSON ARCHIVE p. 31

Colour plates

BELFAST Ulster Museum p. 61: DUBLIN Commissioners of Public Works p. 17: RICHARD HAUGHTON pp. 18 (bottom), 35, 36, 72, 90, 100, 149 (bottom): PAUL SEHEULT p. 168: EDWIN SMITH pp. 89, 167: SPECTRUM COLOUR LIBRARY pp. 62, 71, 99, 150: Courtesy STOPPENBACH AND DELESTE p. 149 (top): CHARLES WALKER p. 18 (top)